CREATIVE ETHICAL PRACTICE IN COUNSELLING & PSYCHOTHERAPY

SAGE has been part of the global academic community since 1965, supporting high quality research and learning that transforms society and our understanding of individuals, groups and cultures. SAGE is the independent, innovative, natural home for authors, editors and societies who share our commitment and passion for the social sciences.

Find out more at: **www.sagepublications.com**

CREATIVE ETHICAL PRACTICE IN COUNSELLING & PSYCHOTHERAPY

Patti Owens, Bee Springwood and Michael Wilson

Los Angeles | London | New Delhi
Singapore | Washington DC

First published 2012

SAGE Publications Ltd
1 Oliver's Yard
55 City Road
London EC1Y 1SP

SAGE Publications Inc.
2455 Teller Road
Thousand Oaks, California 91320

SAGE Publications India Pvt Ltd
B 1/I 1 Mohan Cooperative Industrial Area
Mathura Road
New Delhi 110 044

SAGE Publications Asia-Pacific Pte Ltd
3 Church Street
#10–04 Samsung Hub
Singapore 049483

Library of Congress Control Number: 2011936295

British Library Cataloguing in Publication data

A catalogue record for this book is available from the British Library

ISBN 978-1-4462-0201-2
ISBN 978-1-4462-0202-9 (pbk)

Typeset by C&M Digitals (P) Ltd, Chennai, India
Printed and bound by CPI Group (UK) Ltd, Croydon, CR0 4YY
Printed on paper from sustainable resources

CONTENTS

ABOUT THE AUTHORS

Patti Owens is a psychotherapist, counsellor, supervisor and CPD facilitator with a private practice in north London. Initially trained as a Gestalt psychotherapist, she now adopts an integrative humanistic approach, incorporating object relations and attachment theory. She is a former Board and Ethics Committee member of the UK Association for Humanistic Psychology Practitioners. Her earlier career, which she combined with bringing up a family, was as a primary school teacher and university lecturer – in Arts at the Open University and in Early Childhood Studies at the University of Hertfordshire. She has published articles on ethical issues in psychotherapy and is the editor of *Early Childhood Education and Care* (Stoke on Trent: Trentham Books, 1997).

Bee Springwood originally trained in Art Therapy in 1979, then in Body Psychotherapy, and Psychosynthes is. Her trainings were both psychodynamic and humanistic, and she now works integratively. She is a member of UK AHPP and ex-chair of the Ethics Committee, with a special interest in mediation. Her experience includes work in Children's Services, Mental Health Acute Care, Probation Services, Counselling Centres, Rape Crisis and Drug and Alcohol recovery units. She has been in private practice since 1984, and has been a supervisor and trainer since the 1990s. She co-directed a Diploma in Counselling, and a Group Work Training.

Michael Wilson is a psychotherapist, counsellor (UKAHPP Acc. UKCP Reg.), supervisor, and transpersonal psychology practitioner. He practises in Edinburgh and from his home in Berwick-upon-Tweed, and teaches widely in the field of counselling and psychotherapy in further and higher education. He also offers workshops in the field of transpersonal psychology and related areas in the UK, and sometimes farther afield. He has a longstanding interest in the evolution and practical application of transpersonal psychologies, and is a member of the Confederation for Analytical Psychology, and a former Chair of UKAHPP. His integrative practice is informed by Jungian and eco-psychological perspectives (www.michaelwilson.uk.com).

ACKNOWLEDGEMENTS

We are very grateful to Sydney Bayley, Bridget Grant and James Ryan, experienced psychotherapists, supervisors and trainers, who found time to read our early draft material and provide detailed feedback. We also wish to thank each of our peer professional support networks for time spent on discussing ideas for the book. Sydney Bayley's work on the booklet *Safer Practice Guidance for Psychotherapists* (2009) provided an important initial stimulus for our exploration of therapeutic practice in the text. That, in turn, was inspired by Anne Kearns's supervision course, 'The Seven Deadly Sins', in which Patti Owens and Sydney Bayley were participants. We also wish to thank members of UKAHPP for sparking off ideas that led to the writing of this book, and the organisation itself for giving us permission to reproduce extracts from their ethical codes and procedures. Last, but by no means least, we wish to thank our SAGE editors, in particular Alice Oven for her encouragement and support throughout the book's production.

INTRODUCTION

About this book

This book seeks to address an issue of general concern among counsellors and psychotherapists: how we ensure that our work with clients is both ethical and creative. One key aspect of therapeutic ethics is our capacity to work safely, for the sake of our clients and ourselves as professionals. As counsellors and therapists, we take care to create and maintain a secure, supportive environment for the work we undertake together with our clients. Our professional codes express and support our awareness of the ethical boundaries involved. Effective and ethical boundaries offer a fundamental framework for safe therapeutic process. Creativity – a collaborative activity – is, however, just as essential. Creativity supports movement, transformation, development and change. It also potentially challenges safety. The task of the therapeutic practitioner is to balance the tension between safe structure and creative practice. In this book, we aim to support practitioners in developing and sustaining a practice that is ethical but not rule-bound; creative whilst avoiding careless or reckless action; safe without being professionally or personally defensive. We use the term 'practical wisdom' to express this approach.

We take the view that every practitioner faces ethical issues and is bound to make mistakes from time to time. We believe that these need to be brought fully into professional awareness, rather than being kept hidden and unexamined. Bounded creativity is needed just as much as a creative attitude to boundaries if we are to avoid making mistakes due to lack of awareness. This does not mean that we should practise defensively. Rather, it entails an attitude that sees mistakes, misunderstandings and mis-attunements as a normal and often fruitful part of a therapeutic process. Such a view takes into account that mistakes will happen in therapy and understands that they need to be worked through in a creative and ethical way, providing an opportunity for growth and development.

Throughout the remainder of this book, we use the generic term 'therapist' to mean all those engaged in the work of counselling, psychotherapy and related psychological professions. Similarly, we use the term 'therapy' whenever we are talking about this continuum of professional work, though in individual instances we might specify the kind of professional involved:

counsellor, psychotherapist, and so on. We have tried to keep in mind the range of roles and settings, private and public, in which therapists work, and we have also tried to address therapists at various stages in their careers. Students and trainee therapists in the practitioner phase of training can use the book, and the examples it contains, as a resource for developing their own therapeutic practice. More experienced therapists might use the book as a stimulus and support for reflection on practice and ongoing professional development.

Writing about the process of therapy

A wide variety of actual therapeutic situations are described throughout this book. Whilst the people named in these episodes are not real therapists or real clients, the issues described and discussed are drawn from the authors' own experience as clients, therapists, supervisors and trainers. We call these accounts of therapy 'vignettes'. There are short vignettes which help illustrate an issue being discussed in the course of a chapter; there are also longer vignettes which track therapy over a period of time, providing a basis for a different kind of exploration and enquiry. We prefer not to use the term 'case study' as this implies that the client is the primary object of study, whereas we intend the main focus in each vignette to be on the personal and professional attitudes and behaviours of the therapist. The vignettes are designed to show the therapist's self-awareness as well as their understanding of the client's experience. In this kind of writing about therapy, the client is not an object of study or a pseudo-scientific 'case'. The (fictional) therapist is involved in the process of therapy, not as an outside observer of the client.

As therapists and trainee therapists, readers of this book will understand that in our profession we come to know and work with each client's individuality and personal uniqueness. At the same time, therapist and client learn things together which are often highly revealing of features of experience that many human beings share. Therapists need to hold both the uniqueness of an individual client *and* his or her common humanity. It is important for the client to be recognised as 'who they are' – a wonderful and original whole person. *And* it is often a great relief for the client to know that they share with other human beings similar patterns of personal and interpersonal experience. This is not necessarily to feel categorised or objectified. It is to feel one's individuality *and* one's commonality – fully, relationally, in the core of one's self as a human being. Thus when we use these stories of therapeutic practice and explore them from various theoretical perspectives, using at times different diagnostic and interpretative terms, we are not attempting to label clients or therapists. We aim to show as much respect in writing as we would in the consulting room (Owens, 2007b: 20–9).

A number of our stories of therapy also show how we use supervision – or, as it is termed in Chapter 2, 're-visioning' – to support the continuous and reflective evaluation of our client work. Most therapists are committed to maintaining a supervisory resource as a regular aspect of their personal and professional support. Readers of this book who are also supervisors of other therapists will, we hope, find the issues illustrated and discussed to be of interest to them in that aspect of their work. Supervision teaches us that there is never only one story of a person's therapy. In 're-visioning', we welcome and benefit from our colleagues' contributions, especially as they enlighten and challenge our client work. In a similar way, we invite the reader to engage with the experiences we describe and the issues we discuss over the course of the book.

The 'pause for thought' reflective exercises

This book has been designed to engage you, the reader, in a kind of 'conversation' with the authors. We present our ideas here not as a fully finished study, but as a work in progress and part of a dialogue with other members of our professions. The 'pause for thought' exercises are intended to provide opportunities for you to reflect on matters we are investigating in the book: issues of practising creatively as well as ethically. In keeping with the name we have given them, we urge you to 'pause' in your reading at these points and give some time to the activities and questions suggested, before moving on in your reading of the main text.

A 'pause for thought' may be asking you to compare your own experience with that described in one of our vignettes. It may be offered as a way of encouraging you to consider your own views on a topic that the book is about to discuss, or it might be asking you to read and think about a document included in the resources section at the end of the book. It could be suggesting you try applying some of the ideas explored in the chapter to an experience of your own. It may be a way of highlighting a chapter or book theme, or offering a way of integrating your own learning with one of the perspectives described in the book.

The questions, exercises and activities can be tackled by individual readers or by trainees or practitioners in groups. If you are using the book mainly for personal study you might wish to make notes on a particular 'pause for thought' and use these as a basis for discussion with your supervisor or other interested peers. You will probably gain more from the exercises if you do this. Other readers may find a 'pause for thought' exercise helpful as a resource in their training group or continuing professional development group, or in peer supervision. Whatever the particular purpose, we hope that the 'pauses for thought' will make your reading of this book a more active, engaging, and rewarding experience.

● ● ● *Pause for thought: making a start* ● ● ●

- *Bring to mind one or two experiences in therapy that you have had – as a therapist or trainee therapist, as a client or as a supervisor – which taught you something about (a) creativity in therapy; and (b) safety as an aspect of ethical therapeutic practice.*
- *Jot down a few notes about why you chose those experiences as examples, and what you feel you learned from them, or any questions or issues they raised for you.*

Then read the next section of this Introduction to get a sense of how the book will explore issues of creativity, safety, and 'practical wisdom'.

A brief overview of the rest of the book

The main argument of the book is that ethical practice combines safety and creativity. We take the view that it is the responsibility of practitioners to be personally and professionally aware, to pay attention to ongoing ethical issues in short- and longer-term therapeutic relationships, and to be willing to work things through in the therapy situation with the client, wherever possible.

Chapter 1, 'Contemporary Therapeutic Practice', begins with an exploration of therapeutic ethics, highlighting the process of collaboration that is at the heart of therapy. It argues that a therapist needs 'practical wisdom' in order to balance the demands of ethical and creative work with clients. The chapter discusses some of the tensions between therapeutic ethics and the values of consumer culture, situating the rise in complaints against therapists over recent years in this context, and argues that therapists need to be aware of the possible reasons for complaints in order to practise safely.

Chapter 2, 'Cornerstones of Therapy', explores in more detail the theme of ethical and creative therapeutic practice. It identifies and discusses a number of 'cornerstones' that support good practice: the importance of boundaries; the philosophical and theoretical frame; the primacy of the therapeutic relationship; methodologies and styles of intervention; and the therapist's safe-care system. The chapter invites the reader to reflect on these 'cornerstones' in terms of their underpinning assumptions, with a view to increasing awareness of how together they provide a solid foundation for a practice that is ethical and creative.

Chapter 3, 'Creating and Maintaining Therapeutic Agreements', concentrates on the importance of agreements or contracts between therapist and client. Beginning with the initial agreement, and then exploring how this might be personalised to the individual client, the chapter goes on to look at the need for a review and renewal of agreements over the course of a period of therapy. It concludes by considering the possibility of significant issues arising at the end of a period of counselling or therapy, and what makes for a 'good ending', seen as the expression of a co-created agreement which is coming to completion.

Chapter 4, 'Framing the Therapeutic Process', explores different ways of framing the task and process of therapy: the environmental, contractual and relational frames. These frames overlap and are interconnected, providing clear ethical boundaries for the work. The creative process of therapy is also bounded by the safety these frames provide, as illustrated in the chapter vignettes. The chapter also discusses three 'currencies' – time, money, and self worth – which form part of the meaning-making process between client and therapist.

Chapter 5, 'Dealing with Mistakes in Therapeutic Practice', begins with an acknowledgement that mistakes are inevitable in therapy, and that when dealt with non-defensively they can be opportunities for healing and further growth. The chapter considers some factors which give rise to mistakes and mis-attunements, and offers some thoughts on how these might be minimised. The ethical review procedure as developed by the UK Association for Humanistic Psychology Practitioners (UKAHPP) is discussed as an example of support for safe and creative practice. The chapter then considers how more formal complaints might arise, before looking at the role of mediation in resolving complaints.

Chapter 6, 'Reviewing Your Practice and Looking Forward', consists largely of a 'review questionnaire' designed to help the reader review their own personal and professional experience, in the light of the book's major themes. This review can then be used as a basis for developing the reader's ethical and creative practice as a therapist, whatever their career stage or practice setting.

Writing this book

The production of this book has involved not only drafting written material but also discussing and refining ideas together and rewriting to reflect as much as possible of our critical and collaborative thinking. The three authors have contributed to each other's chapters during the whole process, but Patti Owens is largely responsible for this introduction and for Chapters 1, 3 and 6, Michael Wilson for Chapters 2 and 5, and Bee Springwood for Chapter 4 and the last section of Chapter 5. Patti Owens took overall editorial responsibility for the development of the book.

The use of the pronoun 'we' throughout the text reflects this process of col-laboration, rather than representing a totally uniform authorial line. The authors are all humanistic and integrative therapists, and members of the UK Association for Humanistic Psychology Practitioners (UKAHPP) as well as the United Kingdom Council for Psychotherapy (UKCP), but each comes with a different approach and range of training and experience. Michael Wilson trained first as an integrative counsellor (psychodynamic and person-centred), and then as a transpersonal psychotherapist. His practice is also informed by Jungian and ecopsychology perspectives. Bee Springwood's training has been both psychodynamic/attachment-based and humanistic/transpersonal, and her work includes art psychotherapy, body psychotherapy and psychosynthesis. Patti Owens trained initially as a Gestalt psychotherapist with individuals and groups. She now adopts an integrative humanistic approach that includes insights from developmental psychology and object relations. The writing of the book, we believe, has benefited from the variety of approaches, theoretical perspectives and experience of its authors, and our different 'voices' are evident in the chapters that follow. We hope that this will make for a richer dialogue with a wider range of practitioners than would have been the case had the book been written by a single author.

CHAPTER 1

CONTEMPORARY THERAPEUTIC PRACTICE

Therapy and ethics

It is perhaps the intimately collaborative nature of the therapeutic process and relationship, whether in short- or long-term work, which our clients most value. Collaboration and negotiation are therefore at the heart of therapeutic ethics. Therapist and client, as partners in this project, share the responsibility to engage with each other, to value each others' experience, and to persist through any difficulties that may arise on the way. The therapist makes a commitment to the client's well-being, using his or her professional expertise and personal learning in support of the client.

In this collaborative process there will be moments of absolute meeting between two human beings. There will also be times of difficulty: blocks and misunderstanding to be worked through. Such a journey can not be wholly encapsulated in our professional codes of practice or set down in procedural frameworks. Creativity, spontaneity, risk-taking are part of the therapeutic process. So is the consistent and constant 'holding function' on the part of the therapist who respects the client's need for security and containment (Winnicott, 1990: 240). Our efforts as therapists are directed towards support for the client's development, but we also recognise that the client is the expert on their own lived experience. No amount of professional knowledge and judgement should deter us from valuing this expertise in the client.

In collaborative therapeutic ethics the client's well-being is appropriately balanced with that of their therapist. From this perspective, ethical considerations respect the fundamental equality between two people, therapist and client. Such equality nevertheless sits alongside areas of difference in experience, expertise, personal development and responsibility within the therapeutic dyad. For example, the therapist will expect to take responsibility for their own well-being, as well as that of their client, but the reverse should not be the case. Therapists need to be aware of the sometimes subtle ways in which clients might try to take care of them, so that if necessary this can be given attention in the course of therapy.

The following vignette illustrates how care for a client, therapist self-care, and client autonomy may interact. It includes three different 'possible therapist responses' to the same set of circumstances.

VIGNETTE: 'HILARY AND MALCOLM'

Hilary is a psychotherapist in private practice who sometimes accepts referrals from psychiatric support services in her locality. She has been seeing Malcolm twice a week for six years, since he left hospital following a psychotic breakdown. Since then he has had no further hospitalisations, has found employment in a small furniture factory and has developed a relationship with a woman he met through work. Hilary and Malcolm have been discussing a move to once weekly therapeutic support. Whilst he is keen to do this on one level, he has said he is also afraid that with less support he might become unwell again. Hilary is reflecting on all this whilst waiting for him, and is also looking forward to a walk in the park with a friend, planned later that afternoon. Malcolm telephones to say that his bus has broken down so he will be late and maybe will not get to his session. He sounds very distressed and also reports that he and his girlfriend have had a row that morning.

First possible therapist response

Hilary tells Malcolm that she will be available until the time set for the end of his session and asks him to ring again if he decides to abandon the attempt to come. Putting down the phone, she is pleased that she held the therapeutic boundaries and did not just react to his obvious distress. When he rings again five minutes later to cancel the session she simply reminds him of the date and time of their next planned meeting. She makes a note of the interchange with Malcolm and goes off for her walk. At his session the following week, Malcolm is a bit subdued at first but soon becomes involved in talking about his relationship. Hilary is aware that neither of them has mentioned what had happened the week before. She assumes it has all 'blown over' and is relieved to get back to what she sees as the main business of Malcolm's therapy.

Second possible therapist response

Without giving it too much thought, Hilary suggests that Malcolm should not worry about the time but come when he can and they can time the session from whenever he arrives. She knows that she has no more clients that day, though it will mean cancelling her walk in the park. He eventually arrives 40 minutes late, looking tense and flushed. He expresses his annoyance at being late and his gratitude for Hilary's flexibility. Late in the session Hilary thinks that he has calmed down enough to talk about the row with his partner and how he might try to re-connect with her following the row. Malcolm is effusive in his thanks when he leaves 50 minutes later.

Third possible therapist response

When Malcolm rings, Hilary reminds him that there are still 45 minutes of his session left, so he may well arrive in time for at least a part of the session. She considers offering him a later time as he is obviously distressed, but decides against this as she does not wish to cancel her planned walk. In the event, Malcolm arrives with 25 minutes to spare. He looks tense and flushed, loudly expressing his annoyance at being late and losing half his session 'even though he was paying for all of it'. He switches quickly to talk of the row with his partner but Hilary remains affected by his anger. She interrupts him, saying 'Malcolm, I can't hear you properly because I feel as if you are angry with me. I know you realise that it is not my fault that the bus broke down and made you late. But you seem annoyed about me not being able to offer you a full session, too?' Malcolm replies almost immediately 'I've never been angry with you before, have I?' They go on to talk about his fears that Hilary might not be able to tolerate him being angry with her. He knows his anger had destroyed other relationships. Hilary carries on this work, owning her wariness of his powerful anger but assuring him that she will not be destroyed by him being a bit annoyed with her, or disappointed in her; that was normal in any relationship.

● ● ● *Pause for thought: care, responsibility and autonomy* ● ● ●

- *Which of the three 'possible therapist responses' in this vignette best illustrates the ability to hold these ethical considerations alongside each other: care for the client; therapist self-care; and the client's autonomy and self-responsibility?*
- *What are the features of the therapist's response that led you to say this?*
- *How would you characterise the ethical stance taken by the therapist in the remaining two possible responses?*

The third therapist response perhaps illustrates the most collaborative attitude. This therapist tries to hold the balance between the ethical considerations of care for the client, therapist self-care and the client's autonomy and self-responsibility. There are a number of features of her response that demonstrate this. For example, she keeps her focus on Malcolm's issues without losing sight of her own needs. She holds therapeutic boundaries around time and money without being defensive or rigid in her interactions with Malcolm. She considers Malcolm's therapeutic needs in the context of his development as a person, in particular his need to feel and express emotions in a contained way. She understands that he may be afraid of his own powerful anger because of the negative consequences he has experienced in the past. Nevertheless, we could imagine a supervision session following this episode in Malcolm's therapy where Hilary's supervisor might challenge her 'wariness' of his anger. Perhaps she has her own work to attend to around her experience of 'angry men'? Hilary might also need to adjust to the fact that Malcolm has changed over his years of therapy and now has more self-support and maturity, as evidenced in the contactful way the two of them have now begun to work on these issues. This response, in summary, seems both ethical, in the sense of displaying Hilary's developing wisdom and commitment as a therapist, and creative, in the way she genuinely interacts with her client and recognises the changes he is undergoing as a person.

You will have identified ways in which the first two possible responses differed from the third one. In the first response, Hilary held the time boundary very firmly. Many therapists who emphasise the importance of the therapeutic process and relationship as a holding 'container' might do this. But they would also be likely to ensure that they explored the incident in depth with Malcolm at a subsequent session, unlike Hilary here. In a positive sense, she does no intentional harm and does observe recommended therapeutic boundaries. She keeps within the 'rules' she has absorbed from her professional training and made her own. This is a legitimate way of working, and can also be a perfectly adequate response when we are unsure what to do or feel that we need to discuss a situation further with a colleague or supervisor. Most of us – especially perhaps at the outset of our careers, or when working with a very new client – will have 'followed the rules' in order to make ourselves feel safer. The down side, of course, is that here Malcolm has little opportunity to further his development when Hilary responds so inflexibly. There is little space for his anger in this consulting room. You might say here that Hilary protects herself at Malcolm's expense. She does get her walk in the park, but in allowing the incident to 'blow over' she colludes with Malcolm's fear that his angry emotions must be destructive. He complies with her need to return to therapy as she wants it to be.

It also seems less likely that these issues will be taken to supervision, which of course makes the work less 'safe' in the end. As we will see later on, many complaints made by clients are in fact about relatively trivial-seeming incidents, which the therapist, for whatever reason, has consciously or unconsciously missed or glossed over. For the client seeking a relationship with a therapist who will engage with them as a person, such experiences are far from trivial.

The second possible therapist response seems to err in the opposite direction. A subsequent supervision session might see Hilary, in this case, sharing her reaction to Malcolm's distressed phone call. Perhaps she might see that her response had been over-protective and more related to the 'old Malcolm' than Malcolm as he now is; a much stronger person. Together, Hilary and her supervisor might examine this idea in relation to the fact that Malcolm had been 'panicky and tense', treating her on this occasion as the 'one who would make everything all right'.

Looked at in transferential terms, Malcolm's feeling of 'panic' is generated not only by the actual anxiety of the current situation, but also by previous experiences where he may have had to cope with similarly intolerable anxiety, but perhaps then without anybody present to 'make it all right' and help him handle those intense emotions. In this way he is 'transferring' intense need from unresolved past experiences into the current situation, which really just involves being delayed in getting to see his therapist. He is treating Hilary *as if*, in a sense, she is that longed for 'helping parent'. Hilary's counter transference – here meaning her spontaneous response to the way Malcolm brings his intense relational need to her – is for her to be accommodating, soothing, and protective, *as if* she was indeed Malcolm's much needed 'helping parent'. She does not think enough about her own needs because she is caught up in the transference relationship, rather than the real one, here and now.

Of course, she has been his helper in many ways over the course of time, so it was not unnatural for her protective instincts to be triggered by his sense of fear and danger. But now she might ask whether this could have been explored more with Malcolm. It is possible, for instance, that the row with his girlfriend had reactivated his need for an empathic, available figure in his therapist. They might also have identified Malcolm's 'gratitude' and Hilary's relief and pleasure. As therapists like Melanie Klein have argued, gratitude can be 'prompted mainly by feelings of guilt' about envious or angry feelings towards a caregiver (Klein, 1975: 189). Maybe Hilary was avoiding becoming the target of Malcolm's anger when she decided to be 'flexible'? At any rate, we think you will agree that Hilary here takes an over-caring stance, perhaps because she places caring for the client above her own self-care and an awareness of the client's self-responsibility. This nevertheless distorts her capacity to hold the whole picture in mind and appropriately sustain her professional awareness.

'Practical wisdom' in therapy

As we have seen, there is a balance to be struck between the demands of the therapist's care for the client, the client's self-responsibility and the therapist's self-care. This holding of potentially competing values and demands is part of 'practical wisdom', or what some classical Greek philosophers termed *phronesis* or ethical prudence (Aristotle, 1976: 209–16). With this approach, we do not use our mental capacities to create ethical 'rules' which we then subsequently apply to life situations, separating thinking and reflection from active living. Rather, ethical reasoning is embedded in the actual experiential and practical circumstances of life. Experience causes us to reflect – to take time to consider the meaning of events, experiences, feelings and ideas – and the fruits of our reflection in turn give us wisdom about how to live. The circumstances we encounter generate complex and often competing ethical considerations. Practical wisdom is the capacity to apply ourselves to this particularity and complexity, finding the ethical resolution that seems best in those circumstances. It is a 'resolution' rather than 'solution' because there is not usually a 'right answer' to a complex ethical situation, in the way that, for instance, 'codes of conduct' might suggest. Rather, there is a weighing up of all the ethical considerations in an attempt to act reflectively and wisely.

The concept of practical wisdom is important to us as therapists, because therapeutic ethics originate from our own experience as human beings in relationships. We understand persons to be both individually unique and autonomous *and* intimately interdependent with other people, with community or society, and with the natural world. As we will see in Chapter 2, these ideas are often expressed in professional ethical codes and value frameworks. But by themselves these ideas and values do not guarantee wise action. There is a need for us to engage with the cycle of reflection and experience which can develop our own practical wisdom over time.

Theories of therapy have been generated in just this way. Ever since Freud's groundbreaking work in the nineteenth century, where he offered an explanation for the mental and emotional lives of his patients, therapy theory has grown out of a real engagement with people. The theories can, of course, become quite powerful in themselves, to the point where they assume the status of 'truth' or clinical 'certainty'. This is arguably one factor leading to the rivalries between different therapeutic approaches. But ideally, perhaps, theory can inform therapeutic practice rather than dominate; and practice itself can generate new insights. Each unique situation, and each person's perception of the world, have the potential to contribute to the development of further theory.

Practical wisdom also entails the capacity to live and work with provisional knowledge: the ability to hold uncertainty and adopt a conscious position of 'not knowing'. This attitude complements the therapist's awareness of professional knowledge built up over time, informed by a variety of therapeutic practitioners each with different emphases and understandings about human beings. As therapists we try to hold the whole picture, not judging too soon or discarding whatever does not match some pre-conceived idea. We seek reflection and resolution, rather than solutions which leave out what does not fit. We live and work with uncertainty as therapists, in a world that often encourages us and our clients to split the whole, and to judge what is 'true' or 'right' or 'good' as if these were uncontested ideas, applicable to any circumstance or person.

Let us explore these ideas a little further, by considering this example.

VIGNETTE: 'ELIOT AND ANNE'

Eliot first came to Anne for counselling when his relationship had been disrupted by his partner's sexual infidelity. His partner had also gone to a counsellor on her own account as neither one wished to try couple counselling. Eliot was clear that he wanted to focus on dealing with his 'frightening rage' at what had happened, and needed 'objective input' to help make a decision about whether or not to stay in the relationship. Over the initial weeks, Anne noticed that it seemed to be her role to remind him that he had wanted this focus. Eliot seemed more interested in the exploration of links between his current rage and anger experienced earlier in his life. He also seemed to enjoy discursive conversations with Anne about their very different cultural backgrounds; his in a wealthy, extended Caribbean family and hers in a relatively poor Midlands factory town. Drawing on the ideas of Stephen Johnson, Anne suggested that one way of looking at Eliot's early experience was to see himself as an 'owned child' (Johnson, 1994: 129–53). He had always done what his family expected of him as it was his job to make them proud and happy. This meant that Eliot often felt his desires, hopes and achievements were 'appropriated' by others. He thought that this experience had affected his later life choices, including choices made in his central adult relationship which now made him resentful, driven and something of a martyr to his current family. Together he and Anne reflected on his relative lack of experience of respectful, intimate relationships, as contrasted with intrusive and controlling elements in his developmental relationships. This may have caused him to defend himself against 'invasion', as he saw it.

At the end of a session not long before a planned holiday Eliot surprised Anne by making a request to change from weekly to monthly sessions after the break. Anne suggested they talk more next week, and later took her concerns to supervision. She and her supervisor discussed the work on Eliot's 'owned child' and considered his request in the light of a possible need to control the pace and level of intimacy in the counselling relationship. Anne explored her own feelings of being a bit controlled by Eliot. She was aware of feeling 'on her toes' and 'being kept hard at work'. Was this her own need to 'work hard' in order to feel she was doing valuable work with Eliot? Or was it also, perhaps, a counter transference response – Eliot's 'angry child' who needed to be in control, in a sense making Anne 'work hard'? If so, this might help Anne understand better what it was like for Eliot to feel so driven and 'controlled' in order to feel worthy inside himself. It was important to hold all this in her awareness when deciding how to deal with Eliot's request, so that it did not become a battle for control.

When they met again they reviewed the work so far, recognising that although attention had been given to Eliot's original relationship problem, this remained unresolved. He was still unsure about it, if much calmer than he had been, but said he could live with that for the time being as he had become aware that he had his own questions to deal with. He said he was beginning to recognise that he had never really made choices for himself until recently. He did not want to become a 'resentful – and guilty – old man'. They also considered his need to slow down, wondering if this could be a theme for both of them. Anne shared a little of her experience of 'wanting to be a really good therapist for you' but feeling 'on her toes' sometimes. Eliot laughed and said he was very familiar with that striving in himself. They both agreed it would be good to lessen the pressure, whatever was decided about session regularity.

●● *Pause for thought: practical wisdom in therapy* ●●●

- *Can you identify in this vignette any of the key features of therapeutic ethics, as discussed so far?*
- *How would you say it illustrates the therapist's practical wisdom in development?*
- *Can you bring to mind an experience of your own (with a client, if possible) which illustrates similar features – collaboration, balancing 'goods' or 'truths', holding not-knowing as well as knowing, and so on?*

This example does seem to illustrate some of the key features of therapeutic ethics. The process of therapy is characterised by the collaboration between therapist and client and therapist and supervisor. Anne hears her client's account of himself and his needs in therapy. She engages with Eliot whilst also reflecting on what he says from her own perspective, informed by professional study and supervisory support. There is a process of negotiated meaning-making at the heart of this work (something we will discuss further in Chapter 2). The response to Eliot's request is not presented as a 'right way' or a 'good answer' but is more an acknowledgement of the need to consider the whole picture, as far as possible.

All this illustrates the therapist's developing practical wisdom. You could say that Anne arrives at a resolution to this issue with her client, rather than a solution. Some of the complex layers of meaning are suggested by her own professional understanding and in conversation with her supervisor. She learns, for example, that when she feels 'controlled' by a client this can often be a sign that the client feels, or has felt, controlled at some important point in their own development. But it is with Eliot that she finds a resolution that reflects his insights as well as her own. They both accept his uncertainty about his initial presenting problem; he remains unsure about his relationship with his partner. Eliot himself finds satisfaction in the recognition that his 'frightening rage' is perhaps a necessary process for him in challenging the power of past relationships, as well as being a response to current relational events. The practical 'answer' to Eliot's request – whether or not to change the regularity of his counselling sessions – remains to be decided but both parties are confident that it will be on the basis of this fuller, shared understanding of the issues.

Therapy and consumerism

We have seen so far that there are some key features of therapeutic ethics. These include the process of collaboration and negotiated meaning-making at the heart of therapy. The intention to hold the whole, rather than split off or polarise opinions, views and experiences, seems integral to this enterprise. The therapist's reflective attitude to ethical issues in therapy supports the development of wisdom, rather than mere knowledge, for both client and therapist. Practical wisdom grows out of experience shared, mutually honoured and understood.

These are grounded ideals that inform our work as therapists. But in the UK and perhaps in the developed world more generally, we and our clients are living in a consumer society, which can generate practices that run counter to therapeutic ideals. Therapy is concerned with people as relational human beings, interconnected with each other and the wider world, whereas consumerism focuses on the individual as a 'user' or 'buyer' of things, experiences and people. Therapy, at its best, fosters negotiated, shared meanings and collaboration towards human growth. Consumerism, at its worst, breeds competition, rivalry and an envy of others. The uncertainty that therapists accept as an appropriate response to life's complexity seems to be at odds with the search for 'happiness' or 'success' that is central to consumerism. Being a consumer is supposed to provide us with a sense of security, satisfaction, belonging and happiness. No one wants to be left out of the promise of this experience. As therapists, though, we understand 'the good life' to be one that is based on authentic choices made by the person who continues to discover what gives *their* life meaning. This person aims to lead a 'flourishing' life, rather than a narrowly 'happy' one (Macaro, 2006: 16). We also understand that the 'flourishing' life will usually be a mixed experience. Life will always have ups and downs; some aspects may feel resolved for now and others remain less settled.

Everywhere, it seems, the consumer ethic prevails. Professionals come to be seen as selling a service just as a shopkeeper sells goods to customers. Universities, hospitals, arts events increasingly use the term 'customer' rather than student, patient, audience, participant. Even 'client', our most commonly used term for the people we work with, is a word more redolent of a business arrangement. A glance at some of the current advertising for the variety of therapeutic services on offer highlights the extent to which therapy can be presented as a commodity, to be bought and sold. In plain terms, as therapists and clients we are often caught up in the tensions generated by the fact that we are practising therapy within a consumer context.

The following vignette is an imaginary example based on concerns expressed in many supervision group discussions. Mustapha is a counsellor in a workplace counselling service within a large organisation.

VIGNETTE: 'MUSTAPHA'S STORY'

Many of the clients I work with come to counselling feeling ill with stress or anxiety. They are often on sick leave so they can take the time to come to counselling to 'sort themselves out'. The corporation is paying for the counselling and they supply feedback forms to complete at the end of the series of sessions. They want to know if the client has made good use of the counselling, and in consultation with the client I give feedback about what issues have been covered. First of all, I can see that for most people I work with, the reasons for their stress and anxiety are absolutely plain. Maybe the corporation has made other staff redundant and this has had a direct impact on my client's workload. The anxiety they feel is often the result of pressure put on by managers or other colleagues to complete an impossible workload. The culture is very macho in this corporation. But usually, the client thinks there is something wrong with them for not being able to cope.

How do I respond? Well, I try to understand what the person is experiencing that makes them feel so worried and unable to cope with the work situation. As well as recognising the real, practical, external reasons for their stress and anxiety, we look at how the client reacts. Sometimes this means helping them develop practical coping strategies like finding support with other colleagues and friends. Sometimes we look at how stress can be a disempowering experience because it triggers a child-like memory or behaviour, so the client does not feel or act like an adult. And we work together to give the client a clearer sense of what is their responsibility and what is the manager's, or the employer's, so they see the politics of their problem, if you like. Now and then, the best thing is to help the client to move towards getting out of a toxic situation and finding another job. Even so, I often feel compromised because I'm helping a client to adjust to a less than tolerable situation.

● ● ● **Pause for thought: practising therapy** ● ● ●
in a consumer culture

- *Try to summarise the ways in which Mustapha attempts to hold and resolve the tensions between his therapeutic work and the demands of a consumer culture.*
- *Then, consider how you might have experienced such tensions in your own work. For example, have you ever felt, like Mustapha, 'compromised'?*
- *Finally, have a think about what these experiences suggest concerning tensions that may exist between the practice of therapy and the ideology of the consumer.*

Mustapha's account highlights at least one source of tension. The corporation expects Mustapha to 'fix' this client so he can return to work as a more effective employee. It is, supposedly, the client who has something wrong with him: he cannot cope with the demands of his job, which are deemed to be appropriate. Mustapha, on the other hand, sees the situation in a more complex light. If an aim of therapy is to support his client's well-being, Mustapha may want to help him keep his job and cope more happily with the demands, if possible. But he also feels 'compromised'. There is often, he seems to think, a tension between his clients' authentic personal awareness of distress and lack of fulfilment, and the emphasis on success and money-making which defines consumer culture, rather than meaning-making. Mustapha does employ practical wisdom in prioritising his clients' well-being within a context that arguably does not offer enough support. He finds a way, with his clients, of reaching a provisional resolution of their immediate concerns. And even so he feels 'compromised'.

We wonder what experiences of this kind you might have had. Maybe you will have identified with the tension Mustapha feels between the aim of supporting his client to develop awareness, responsibility and choice as a person and the pragmatic need to help him adjust to a less than life-enhancing workplace situation. You might also have identified other tensions which arise when your core therapeutic values are challenged. Like Mustapha, you and your client may sometimes be asked to report to a third party who in a sense 'owns' the therapy because they are paying for it. This can set up a tension between your basic confidentiality boundaries and the knowledge that this is the only way your client is going to get any therapeutic support at all. What do you do? Our guess is that like Mustapha, you try to find a way to resolve the tensions in a necessarily imperfect manner, attempting to support your clients in the best possible way in those circumstances.

Practising therapy ethically, creatively – and 'safely'

Complaints made to their professional organisations against therapists have been increasing in recent years. For example, in the ten-year period from 1996 to 2006, the British Association for Counselling and Psychotherapy (BACP) received a total of 142 complaints against members, of which 77 went to a full complaints hearing (Khele et al., 2008: 131). Figures provided to the authors of the present book in May 2011 by the BACP reveal that in the ensuing four-year period, from 2007 to 2010, there were 52 complaints hearings. This represents a rise from an average of seven or eight complaints hearings a year, to 13 – quite an increase.

It is important to keep this in perspective. These numbers represent only a tiny fraction of the numbers practising as counsellors, psychotherapists, or in related fields. Even so, the impact of a complaint on individual therapists – and their clients, and the professional organisation involved – is potentially extremely damaging. A lot of therapists find it hard to resume practice following the completion of a professional complaint process (Casemore, 2001: 9–17). Increasingly, it seems, many therapists, and clients, know of someone who has been caught up in a complaint procedure. Working within an atmosphere of potential complaint can have an adverse effect on our professional attitudes unless we open these up to scrutiny.

There are various possible reasons for the rise in the number of complaints against therapists. First of all, there are many more therapists in practice in the UK than there were 20 years ago, and a much larger percentage of the UK population is now having some experience of psychological therapy. This increase is partly due to health initiatives such as the Improving Access to Psychological Therapies programme (IAPT) which has trained over 3,000 new cognitive behavioural therapists to deal with the 491,000 new clients offered treatment by Primary Care Trusts (www.iapt.nhs.uk/). Given the greater numbers of people engaging in therapy, it is not in itself surprising that the overall number of complaints against therapists has risen.

We might also consider a second factor in this apparent rise in complaints: the consumer culture that we looked at in the last section. The consumer, or 'customer', expects to be able to buy a guaranteed product. People are also less likely to put up with poor standards or service; expectations are rising. There is a whole vocabulary of complaint handling which emphasises and often polarises two concepts. On the one hand, there is the responsibility of the service provider to deliver a good service to customers or clients. On the other hand, if the client or customer does not receive the service they expect they can make a complaint, usually to a person or body deemed to be a 'higher authority'. There is now a society-wide apparatus of law and institution set up with the purpose of investigating and adjudicating complaints. Every organisation, small and large, has its complaints procedures, officers and departments. This is mirrored in the many different complaints procedures found among the wide variety of UK therapy's individual professional organisations.

Whatever the societal reasons for the rise in complaints, it is perhaps more important to consider in some detail the nature of the complaints, and factors that are specific to our profession. In a study carried out in 2008 by John Monk-Steel, Chair of the United Kingdom Council for Psychotherapy (UKCP) Registration Board, he concluded that though the most serious complaints concern sexual or physical abuse, the vast majority of cases are concerned with relatively minor 'relational' issues between client and therapist. He summarised these issues as arising from:

- misunderstandings between client and therapist;

- lack of a shared perspective;

- mistakes on the part of the therapist that have gone unacknowledged;

- projections not owned, but acted out by client or therapist;

- unconscious or unaware feelings, especially envy, hostility or erotic attraction.
  (Monk-Steel, 2009: 3)

As we will explore in Chapter 5, these relational issues, though in one sense 'minor' because they do not lead to serious physical harm or sexual abuse, are nevertheless highly significant when things go wrong in therapy. A misunderstanding or mistake on the part of the therapist can be experienced very intensely by a client seeking a healing or reparative relationship. Real emotional harm can be done to a client by a therapist who remains unaware of the kind of unconscious feelings Monk-Steel identifies. These are often just the kinds of issues that emerge when a complaint is made. Unfortunately it is sometimes then too late to repair the damage caused, wittingly or unwittingly, within the therapeutic relationship.

Furthermore, other research has suggested that there may be a significant subset of clients whose psychological profile makes them more likely to complain against their therapists. These are clients whose 'fragile self-process' also exhibits characteristics of complex post-traumatic stress disorder (Kearns, 2007: 40–2). They may also have been involved in complaints against other professionals. Kearns argues that these clients are over-represented amongst therapy complainants. It seems that such clients may be particularly vulnerable to forming the impression that their therapist is deliberately doing them harm whenever they experience a violation of personal security boundaries in therapy.

One example, based on an actual complaint case examined in recent years, might suffice to illustrate Kearns's point. The complaint centred on the therapist's giving the client a parting gift at the end of a period of therapy. The therapist saw this as a mark of respect for the client and the value of work undertaken over several years in therapy. The complaining client, on the other hand, saw the gift as representative of a shift in the therapist's relational boundary from therapist to 'friend'. This made the client frightened: significant boundaries had been broken in the client's previous life with tragic consequences. At the time of the gift-giving the client had felt unable to tell their therapist of these fears as they did not wish to be thought 'ungrateful' at this sensitive ending time in therapy. Three years later, the client made a formal complaint to the therapist's professional organisation and the complaint was upheld.

Kearns would argue that therapists need to know the risks involved in working with clients with a fragile self-process. We need the capacity to work with such clients' unconscious as well as conscious material, which requires effective supervision, personal development, professional knowledge and competent practice. But there is another possibility that we need to think about: that the 'fragile self-process' of therapists can also influence the situation. As Kearns remarks, 'effective psychotherapists need to accept and get to know their fragile parts', in the understanding that the 'self-process is essentially fragile' (2005: 25–7). Robert Lee also points out that many of us have had experiences of loss, trauma, discrimination, hardship of various kinds, which may result in us projecting 'significant parts of our self – our affects, desires, ways of being in the world' onto our clients (Lee, 2004: 339). Is it possible that in our example the gift-giving therapist thought their client needed a gift as a final valuing gesture, when this was in fact the therapist's own need? Had the gift been given earlier, and not in the final session, there might have been an opportunity for this potential muddle to be resolved, and the therapist's own self-process acknowledged as contributing to the client's experience of being ill-recognised in their need for firm boundaries.

Daniel Stern's pioneering (1985) research, based on detailed observations of infants with their primary carers and conversations with those carers, did much to connect an interpersonal view of human development with the relational nature of reparative and healing psychotherapy. Lee takes a similarly relational perspective on human development and on therapy, arguing that we form our selves in our interaction with others. My self-process affects yours, and vice versa. These writers take the view that human development happens in relationship. It is also 'layered', involving strands of development that emerge at different points in the therapy. With this view, development is not 'completed' when childhood issues are resolved. Rather, we go on developing throughout life. Therapy offers a primary arena for this relational life work, affecting both client and therapist (Philippson, 2001: 211). All this indicates a need for therapists to have awareness and responsibility for their own 'fragile self-process', especially as differently experienced with each client. One therapist gives the following account of this:

> I always ask myself, and my supervisor will often ask me as a reminder, just how I experience being with this client? What do I feel and think when I am with them – physically, in my body, as well as emotionally and mentally? What is my 'image' or 'snapshot' or 'headline' regarding this client and the way I feel with them?
>
> Over time, I've learnt that when I find myself trying very hard to please or to impress, my own 'grandiose' self-process is being activated. I'm probably dealing with a client who may have had to impress significant people with their hard work in order to get approval or love. Alternatively, if I feel intensely drawn into a client's story, especially if I'm tempted to step over conventional therapeutic boundaries to help or accommodate the client, I'm probably with a person who needs to evoke my 'rescuer' because they don't know how else to deal with intense emotional experiences.

It is not that this therapist's interpretations of her counter-transference responses to clients are necessarily 'correct' or even capable of being generalised. The point is that the therapist knows something about how she typically reacts to different kinds of self-process in her clients. Arguably, this therapist is more likely to be able to use that knowledge to support a client to heal and change, rather than have them repeat a distressing relational experience from the past – either the client's past, or the therapist's.

In this section, to summarise, we have been exploring some of the possible reasons for an increase in complaints against therapists in recent years. There are more therapists practising and many more clients seeking therapy than 20 years ago. The complaints culture and consumer context of our work may also be a contributory factor. Added to this, we may need to develop more awareness of why some clients make formal complaints about relatively minor matters, rather than addressing conflicts more directly with their therapist. All this suggests that a greater priority be given to professional understanding of the relational field of therapy, and the self-process of both client and therapist as they affect the work.

A further factor underlying complaints is that we may not have a deep enough understanding of the ethical potential in our work with clients. We might be familiar with the words used in our various professional ethical codes, without us ever having fully developed and integrated a real appreciation of concepts like 'beneficence' or 'autonomy'. We might not have considered how these values need to be applied to ourselves as well as our clients. We might also not have seen that these values sometimes conflict in a given situation. As the next chapter will indicate, such an understanding comes with our reflection on therapeutic experience – a central argument of this book. Later chapters will ask you to think in detail about aspects of the ethical framework of therapy, and to note how your own values relate to those expressed in the code of ethics for your own professional organisations.

Pause for thought: possible responses to the 'complaints culture'

- Take a moment to check how you have been feeling as you read the previous section about the possibility of complaints being made against therapists. Try to pinpoint your reactions without censoring them, if working alone. If you are in a group, discuss and compare your responses.
- Then look at the following responses from therapist participants in a workshop entitled 'Practising Safely in a Complaints Culture', and compare your responses with theirs.

Therapist 1

'I know the effect all this talk of complaints has on me. I try to stick to the rules of my professional organisation. I observe therapeutic boundaries quite tightly. I only keep minimal records. I don't see clients in my own home but work at a centre where I feel less vulnerable because it is more obviously an institutional setting.'

Therapist 2

'I know complaints happen. I've read about some of them in the professional journals and I actually knew someone in my supervision group who went through a complaint procedure. But I just can't think too much about it. I don't imagine any of my clients would complain. If they did, I don't know what I'd do, so I don't let myself get too preoccupied about it.'

Therapist 3

'I refuse to be intimidated by the possibility of complaint. Clients know when they come to work with me that they are responsible for themselves and must tell me if they don't like what I'm saying or doing. I don't like being tied down to some generalised professional code with its rules and regulations, though I do belong to a professional organisation. I'm responsible for my own practice.'

You may have noticed similar feelings of anxiety or rebellion, confusion or concern, as you were reading this chapter. In our experience these reactions are very common in continuing professional development situations, once the topic of possible complaints against therapists is raised.

The first response above illustrates the more compliant therapist who errs on the side of caution. This therapist has a tendency to stick to the 'rules' and not take chances, which is very understandable. The down side might be that their professional responsibility, creativity and flexibility are diminished. It may be less likely, too, that they would encourage clients to consider the broader options available to them, preferring instead to support their conformity and adjustment to a more limited sphere of life choices.

The therapist in the second response adopts the 'ostrich position' and trusts to something more like 'luck' or chance. This therapist does not show much reflection or 'practical wisdom', and does not seem to involve clients creatively in paying attention to potentially difficult issues. Their unwillingness to consider the possibility of complaint arguably makes them more likely to miss experiences that might in fact lead to the client complaining. In this respect, this therapist is less 'safe' than the first.

The third respondent is something of a maverick. This therapist does have a strong sense of equality between themselves and their client, but seems to pay little heed to the differences of power inherent in the therapeutic relationship. Clients who feel powerless sometimes wait for years after the event to bring a complaint. Such clients might appropriately feel that they have no other recourse but to take formal action, as there is little sense of dialogic space in the therapeutic relationship.

Most of us – and we the authors include ourselves in this – will recognise the fear, dismay, compromised compliance or rebellion expressed by these therapists. Yet as professionals committed to our own and our clients' well-being, we need to continue to maintain and develop our abilities to self-regulate our work. As therapists, we have a responsibility to introduce our clients to the therapeutic approach we take and convey our understanding of the way therapy works as a collaborative enterprise, using both therapist and client expertise and experience. The narrative and discussion in the rest of this book is designed to help you in this. In Chapter 2, reflection on the 'cornerstones' of therapy can support you in articulating more clearly to clients the process and possible outcomes of therapy; what boundaries are; what this means for the way you work together. Any therapeutic agreement or contract you make can then grow out of a shared understanding, as Chapter 3 makes clear. The therapeutic relationship, as Chapter 4 will suggest, can be warm, intimate, creative and supportive and still work within important 'frames' that bound the work of therapy. And in the event that misunderstandings or disputes do arise between therapist and client, these matters might then more often be resolved with respect for the therapeutic process of the client and less often by recourse to legalistic complaints procedures, as Chapter 5 illustrates.

Chapter summary

This chapter has highlighted some of the features of therapeutic ethics, looking at the relationship between reflection and action, thinking and doing. It has argued that therapists need to develop and exercise 'practical wisdom' in order to practise ethically, creatively, and therefore effectively. It has looked at some of the tensions existing between the values of therapy and our consumer culture, situating the rise in complaints in this context. Lastly, it has affirmed that practising 'safely' does not imply defensive or therapist-protective practice. Instead, it requires a steady appraisal of possible reasons why complaints occur and a willingness to engage with these issues from a professionally competent and creative position.

Further reading

Anderson, S.K. and Handelsman, M.M. (2010) *Ethics for Psychotherapists and Counsellors: A Proactive Approach*. Chichester: Wiley-Blackwell. A lively, resource-filled exploration designed to support the reader in defining and developing their own ethical therapeutic framework.

Macaro, A. (2006) *Reason, Virtue and Psychotherapy*. Chichester: Whurr Publishers. This develops the ideas of Aristotle in the modern therapy context. The second chapter focuses on the idea of 'Practical Wisdom: The Art of Making Good Decisions'.

Nicholas, M.W. (1994) *The Mystery of Goodness (and the Positive Moral Consequences of Psychotherapy)*. New York and London: W. W. Norton. Nicholas argues that for a client – or therapist – 'getting better' necessarily involves them in becoming more ethically aware and self-responsible.

Palmer-Barnes, F. (1998) *Complaints and Grievances in Psychotherapy*. London and New York: Routledge. This offers a succinct survey of the history and development of complaints handling in four major professional organisations, highlighting the issues raised for therapists and clients.

CHAPTER 2

CORNERSTONES OF THERAPY

Balancing safety and creativity

Cornerstones, or foundation stones, provide the supportive structure and framework upon which everything rests and relies. Cornerstones of therapy are informed by values, principles, attitudes, beliefs, and ideas which translate into the theory and practice of therapy. Different therapeutic traditions and modalities bring distinctiveness to these cornerstones, depending on what is considered helpful to the therapeutic endeavour and form of treatment. Reflective practice based on these cornerstones makes for effective therapy. However, the relational nature of therapy also means that the therapist must be open to the values and beliefs of the other, which may be different from one's own, and be prepared to engage in non-defensive dialogue about their respective differences. In therapy, two people are engaged in a commitment to ease the suffering and enable the meaning-making process of one of them. It is likely that within this relational field or 'frame', as we discuss in Chapter 4, both people will be changed by the process. Cornerstones, then, form the framework within which this transformation occurs.

The cornerstones we shall discuss are: the philosophical and theoretical frame; boundaries; the therapeutic relationship; methodology or interventions related to the frame; and the therapist's need for self-care. It is the consistency of this framework which contributes to safe therapy. By 'safe' we mean that the therapy is grounded and bounded by the cornerstones. It is this which provides a 'good enough' (Winnicott, 1971: 81) and dependable facilitative environment, and a 'secure base' (Bowlby, 2003: 46) within which the client is able to grow, develop, resolve difficulties and dilemmas, ease suffering, and make meaning.

Of course, clients often bring their own issues around safety and safety-seeking: they might, for example, have difficulties with trust. These may or may not be met by the sense of security which a particular practitioner can provide. Similarly, therapists themselves might have concerns around safe practice and with it sometimes the fear of complaint, which can lead to fear-based defensive practice. Defensive practice can also be a consequence of the therapist's own incomplete awareness. But for therapy to be fully effective it is necessary for it to be more than safe. It must also be creative. The use of the term 'creative' here is distinct from the engagement of clients' creativity in the arts therapies. Being a creative therapist might mean, for instance, using innovative and spontaneous therapeutic interventions, which relate to the specific therapeutic needs of the client in the moment. The argument of this book is that neither 'safe' nor 'creative' practice is effective on its own: both dimensions are necessary for a satisfactory therapeutic outcome.

There is a fundamental connection between safety and creativity in terms of the therapist's motivation to form an authentic connection, or moment of meeting, with the client. However, there is also an inherent tension between safety and creativity. What is considered safe is often in relation to what is known, familiar, and contained, and what is considered creative is often in relation to what is unknown, spontaneous, and may feel uncontained. As therapists, we need to find and be able to hold a balance between a practice which is defensive, 'tight', controlled, and *too* safe on the one hand, and a practice which is relaxed, 'loose', unbounded, and *too* creative on the other.

One way to construe this balance is as a horizontal figure of eight, with 'safe' on the one side, and 'creative' on the other, in a moving dynamic. Sometimes safety is too dominant, while at other times creativity is too dominant, and the reasons for this might relate to the client, the therapist, the process between the two, and/or the context in which the therapy takes place. Figure 2.1 illustrates the figure of eight dynamic. The arrows indicate movement. Sometimes the movement is more towards 'safe', while at other times the movement is more towards 'creative'. This means that the loops are not always of equal size.

To consider what Figure 2.1 looks like in practice, here is an exercise to help you explore the 'both safe and creative' dynamic.

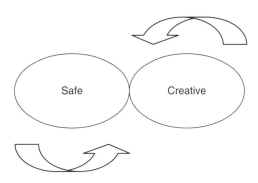

FIGURE 2.1

●●● *Pause for thought: 'both safe and creative' practice* ●●●

- *First, form a large figure of eight on the floor with a long piece of string. Begin by making the two sides symmetrical. Now, take three pieces of paper marked 'safe', 'both/and', and 'creative', and place them in their respective positions in relation to the figure of eight.*
- *Then, think of a client you are currently working with and take up a position on the figure of eight that most expresses your feeling about your work with that client. (Adjust the balance of your figure of eight accordingly.) Consider what it might be in the therapeutic process that gives rise to this 'position'. Then try thinking of a different client and notice what changes and why. Take time to enter into the felt experience of each position.*
- *Consider some of the dilemmas, challenges, difficulties, and possible benefits which you might encounter in either the 'safe' and 'creative' positions.*
- *Finally, consider the benefits and challenges of the 'both/and' position. If you are able to conduct this exploration with a colleague, you might perhaps discuss the similarities and differences of your experiences.*

The issues you have been reflecting on here have very practical implications. For example, a therapist working with abuse issues in an NHS setting might find him- or herself leaning towards 'too safe' practice for obvious reasons. Equally, a therapist who decides that physically holding a client may be therapeutically useful, could in most circumstances be considered as being 'too creative' or unbounded. Sometimes being too creative is unsafe, just as being too safe is uncreative. Both safe *and* creative are necessary in measures appropriate to the unique therapeutic need. Bringing attention to 'both/and' is a necessary challenge for the effective practitioner. Both/and-ness is largely determined by therapeutic need, but is also informed by the therapist's capacity to hold a non-dogmatic position in relation to the five cornerstones of therapy.

The philosophical and theoretical frame

Turning our attention to the cornerstones of therapy, we begin with a consideration of the philosophical and theoretical frame. This cornerstone informs the therapeutic relationship and process, and sets limits around what we are trained to do or not do. It has several components, the first of which centres on those values, principles, beliefs, and assumptions which give distinctiveness to the therapeutic modality. These underpin:

- the therapist's way of relating to the client (*this is how I am going to be with you*);

- the therapist's way of understanding the client (*this is what will inform my thinking about you*);

- the therapist's view of human nature and development (*this is what I think being authentic, healthy, or fully functioning means*).

A second component of our philosophical and theoretical frame provides a theoretical way of viewing:

- the client (*this is the theoretical perspective within which I can begin to understand you*);
- the therapist (*this is how I can begin to understand myself in relation to you*);
- the dynamic relationship between them (*this is how I can begin to understand what's going on between us*).

A third aspect concerns methodology or interventions (verbal and non-verbal) which the therapist uses (*this is how I will interact with you*). Finally, our philosophical and theoretical frame also underpins our perspective on:

- aetiology (*this is how we collaboratively formulate or diagnose your difficulties*);
- treatment (*based on what we have agreed together, this is how I might best help you*);
- the healing process (*this is what I believe healing means, and how it works*).

Pause for thought: values underpinning therapy

- *Take some time to make a list of the values which you think underpin therapy.*
- *How do these values relate to the points above – your way of relating to the client; your way of understanding the client; your view of human nature and development?*
- *Consider how your values and assumptions might be different from a colleague's or a fellow trainee's.*

Your list of therapeutic values will probably reflect not just your professional training and development, but also your life experience more broadly. Because of that, your list is unlikely to be exactly the same as that of a peer or colleague. Even so, you might have included, in your list of values, words such as 'integrity' and 'humility'. To act with integrity in therapeutic practice means not only that you allow the other to be the other, but also that you support the other to develop 'be-ing', as well as applying that value towards yourself. Humility in this context means being 'earthed' enough to recognise that you may not know first or best what might suit the client, but that you are willing to discern this with them. Also, through the levelling which humility brings, comes a recognition of one's own brokenness, and an awareness that 'brokenness' is common to most people. It is from this awareness of common kinship that an authentic meeting is often possible.

The different components which constitute the philosophical and theoretical frame form a dynamic interrelated system, which is continually being researched, fine-tuned, developed, and updated in the light of what is considered therapeutically beneficial. This is the core of a therapeutic model, from which arises the style of the therapeutic relationship and the methodology and interventions that sit congruently within this model. It is a meaning-making system, or framework, within which the therapist is able to make sense of the client's experience. But as such it has influence on how the client begins or continues to make sense of their life. It offers possible reasons for their sufferings or difficulties, and ways of thinking about this.

As Peter Lomas (1999) points out, therapy is not a neutral process. There is no doubt that the therapist's values and way of being, communicated verbally and non-verbally, are introjected or taken in consciously and unconsciously by the client. Even minimal communications like nodding or frowning can potentially convey a value such as 'I agree' or 'I disagree', which has the potential to influence. Similarly, the interpretive and facilitative, or enabling system which the therapist adopts is also highly influential. This is a 'system' or 'core theoretical model' with which the therapist identifies and frequently defends as 'the truth'. Actually, there are many truths. One of the exciting things about integrative practice – bringing together different considered 'truths' into a more-or-less consistent whole – is that it takes seriously the idea that therapy is an evolving open system.

A meaning-making process sits either within a closed system which filters everything through already held values, principles, and beliefs, or within an open system which is allowing and welcoming of newness, the novel, and the unexpected, or somewhere in the middle. An open system embraces the idea of something which continues to unfold, and which will inevitably contain paradoxes. The practitioner who prefers to adopt a more open-system attitude toward the meaning-making process is more likely to be subject to change in the pursuit of truth. To this extent, the pursuit of professional truth sits alongside, and often crosses into, the pursuit of personal truth. This seamless join between person and practitioner is why therapy is often considered to be a vocation or profession rather than a job. It also explains why we place equal value on personal and professional development in the training and on-going accreditation of therapists. The following exercise invites you to think about your own experience of personal and professional development.

⦿⦿⦿ *Pause for thought: the relationship between personal* ⦿⦿⦿
and professional development

- *Take some time to reflect on how your personal development has influenced your development as a therapist, or the way you have worked with clients.*
- *Then take the other perspective, and think about ways in which your professional work has influenced your personal development.*
- *Can you think of ways in which this interaction between personal and professional development might have shaped or clarified some of the values you identified in our earlier 'pause for thought'?*

Personal therapy is an integral part of the preparation and formation of a therapist, and may even be considered to be a cornerstone of effective practice in its own right. The process enables the evaluation and deepening of values, and the promotion of insight and awareness. The therapist's therapist also offers a model of being in the therapeutic relationship. Conversely, as Patrick Casement reminds us in the dedication of his *On Learning from the Patient* (1985) – 'To the many who have helped me learn' – there is a lot to be learnt from the client. For instance, the capacity of individuals to endure through life's adversities, to pull through the deepest wounding, to make astonishing life-changing decisions as well as, sadly, life-ending ones, often has a profound influence on the therapist. Sometimes this means a shifting of one's own values. Being witness to the narrative of people's lives, while often difficult, is also deeply humbling.

Boundaries in therapeutic practice

Therapy is an interaction which takes place within the parameters of specific boundaries. The message which boundaries give is: 'This is how I am going to take care of you, of me, and of the therapeutic space'. First, *you*, because the therapy is for you, and my duty of care is towards you. Second, *me*, because your therapy also includes and will affect me, and a duty of care extends from me to me. Third, *the therapeutic space*, because without a protected space your safety cannot be guaranteed, which means therapy cannot take place. For the beginner as well as for the seasoned practitioner, this may mean ensuring not only that the space is free of external intrusions – such as people coming into the room or being able to see through a window, or disturbance from the ringing of mobile phones – but also that the space or environment is constant and does not change without a prior conversation. This is particularly important for clients who have not experienced some form of healthy constancy of environment, either relational or physical, in life.

Certain boundaries will have been set by the professional body to whose codes or frameworks you subscribe. These will be reiterated and developed by your training organisation, in professional literature which explicitly or implicitly informs you of boundaries, and through discussions with your supervisor, with colleagues or in professional forums. In this section there are three boundaries which we would like you consider more fully. These are the boundaries of ethics, competence and supervision.

The boundary of ethics

As Chapter 1 began to explore, ethical therapeutic practice takes place within a relational frame. It is clear that relational ethics inform our way of being and doing in therapy, and are expressed in our values, frameworks and codes. This has been written about at length by Lynne Gabriel and Roger Casemore (2009), Peter Lomas (1999), and others. Absorbing and integrating the insights gained from the collaborative therapeutic relationship, as we have been arguing, contributes towards making therapy safe.

The ethical codes and frameworks of many professional organisations (for example, the BACP) are based on the following principles.

- *Non-maleficence*: this term derives from the Latin maxim *primum non nocere*, which means 'first, do no harm'. It follows from this that the therapist is required to practise in a bounded, competent and non-exploitative way.

- *Beneficence*: the therapist is committed to working towards increasing the well-being of the client and creating beneficial outcomes. With this in mind, the therapist frequently monitors and improves their practice through self-reflection, supervision and ongoing training and development.

- *Justice*: the therapist practises within legal guidelines, and in a way which respects the client's basic human rights and dignity. A commitment to fairness and equality of opportunity requires the therapist to appreciate differences between people and to honour the obligation not to discriminate in terms of such things as religion, class, political belief, race, ethnicity, gender, sexual orientation, ability.

- *Autonomy*: the therapist is committed to respecting and enabling the client's capacity for self-determination in relation to decision making. We embrace our fullest integrity when we exercise our capacity to make our own decisions, and learn from the consequences of these.

- *Fidelity*: at the heart of fidelity is a commitment to guard the client's disclosures and process, and not unnecessarily disclose these to anyone. It also means keeping promises and upholding the value of honesty in relation to the therapeutic process.

- *Respect*: this goes right to the core of valuing the other. Respect allows the client to be other without the therapist intending to control or manipulate in any way. Respect values the integrity of the other, the client. We need an awareness, however, that our therapeutic values and assumptions can in themselves result in 'manipulation' if they are not open to exploration and discussion with the client.

- *Self-respect*: this principle means that the therapist appropriately applies all the above principles as rights to her- or himself. The attitude inherent in self-respect is the capacity to take oneself into account, and to embody the values of self-kindness and self-compassion (Neff, 2011: 42–60).

As well as these relational ethics there are also practical ethics. For instance, it is an ethical requirement to make sure that your professional liability insurance is kept up to date and that you know what these documents contain, and that you have a therapeutic executor, someone who, in the event of your illness or death, would take care of your clients (see Resource 9, pp. 115–16). These practical issues will be taken up more fully in later chapters.

The boundary of competency

Another key boundary is therapist competency. There is a tendency amongst some therapists to want to appear more capable than they actually are. The truth is that sometimes the therapist's own pathology becomes visible and gets in the way of therapy. Knowing the limits of our competency may lead us to seek more professional support, or to go further into professional development. It takes awareness of our competency to stay where we are until we have engaged fully with, and integrated, any areas of new growth. For instance, it is not ethical for a therapist to spend a few weekends on dream work, and then say that they are now proficient in working with dreams. The same applies to the idea of working with couples, using mindfulness practice techniques, dealing with serious mental illness, or taking therapy into nature. No therapist should engage in such work without sufficient training and experience.

Nick Totton offers a useful insight into what we might call a more general therapist incompetence when he writes that 'humanistic practitioners are perhaps especially vulnerable to charismatic over-generosity, shifting boundaries to "meet the client's needs" (for example around session times, phone calls and texts, and fees) in ways that may actually be destabilising for them' (2010: 50). Therapists can also abandon their competence due to illness, economic necessity, or a tendency to 'rescue' clients, as we shall see in Chapter 5.

● ● *Pause for thought: going beyond the limits of competency* ● ● ●

- *Consider an occasion where you might have been tempted to go beyond your own competency boundary. Maybe you knew you did not have sufficient training as yet to carry out work with this client? Or perhaps excitement at some new learning led you to experiment in a slightly unsafe way in your work?*
- *Did you discuss this with anyone else at the time? If so, what was their response? If not, do you now feel that you should have?*

It is always possible to go beyond our own competency boundary, as the following vignette illustrates.

VIGNETTE: 'POLLY AND DAVID'

Polly was a fourth-year trainee psychotherapist. She had just completed the required mental-health unit placement, attending ward rounds with a psychiatrist at a local hospital. She had become interested in the ways therapy might be helpful in the treatment of psychiatric disorders. By chance, she met a prospective new client, David, who told her straightaway that he had bi-polar disorder. Polly was keen to try out her new learning and agreed to take him on as a client. David seemed to respond well over the initial weeks but then began to behave as if he was entering a period of hyper-activity and hyper-emotion – a 'manic' period. At this point, Polly realised that she was out of her depth and could not support David properly. With the help of her supervisor, she decided to contact his psychiatrist and David was admitted to hospital for a time, and then referred on to therapeutic support within the hospital setting. Polly realised that she should have discussed David's issues with her supervisor during the assessment period, and should probably have referred him on to a more experienced professional. Also, it would have been appropriate to have sought permission from him to set up a communication channel with his psychiatrist and other support services, in this way supporting both people in the process. The crisis could have been avoided if she had not gone beyond her own competency boundary.

A safe and creative therapist knows what it means to practise within the limits of their competency. This might necessitate delaying our engagement in a new area of work with clients until we know that we have fully assimilated a new training. The effective therapist will recognise when it is appropriate to refer a client on to another, more experienced practitioner, which might be considered at any point during the course of therapy. Supervision is also one of the contexts for an exploration of competency and the integration of new approaches, and it is to this that we now turn.

The boundary of supervision

Supervision, or perhaps we should call it 're-visioning', is a boundary because without it the process of therapy would not be ethical. We prefer the term 're-visioning' because this describes more accurately what supervision actually does. It also differentiates this professional, therapeutic relationship and process from other, more hierarchical forms of supervisory support. We understand re-visioning as seeing *with* or *alongside* rather than over-seeing, which the term 'supervision' usually means. Three forms of re-visioning familiar to therapists are:

- *Intrapersonal re-visioning* which often consists of the therapist monitoring their own therapeutic process and relationship, in the moment, in the therapy session, from within. We sometimes refer to this process as developing our own 'internal supervisor'.

- *Interpersonal formal re-visioning* which is the more familiar process of re-visioning with someone more experienced than yourself.

- *Interpersonal informal re-visioning* which consists of meeting peers with a view to developing each other's therapeutic practice, as in a peer supervision or training group, case colloquium, or other forum.

It is worth considering whether or not you have the right balance of these 're-visioning' activities at any stage in your practice. This balance will change over time and in response to your personal and professional development needs. Making adjustments as necessary in your supervision and peer-learning arrangements will strengthen safety boundaries whilst also enriching opportunities for creative growth, for you as a therapist and for your clients. The following example illustrates the use of supervision to consider ways forward in relation to a difficult issue.

VIGNETTE: 'ELIZABETH AND MARY'

During an initial assessment meeting with a new client, the client asked Elizabeth whether it would be all right to tape-record subsequent sessions. Despite her awareness that this was ethically allowable, if they so chose, Elizabeth felt uneasy about the request, and asked that she be allowed to think about it until their next appointment.

   During their 're-visioning' her supervisor, Mary, helped Elizabeth to explore her feelings, and in particular her resistance, in relation to the client's request. What emerged during the re-visioning process was an insight into the nature of confidentiality. At one point during the conversation Mary remarked: 'The confidentiality includes you, Elizabeth'. At this point Elizabeth realised that recording the sessions could inhibit the flow of conversation, which might occasionally include information about Elizabeth herself, in the moment, or exceptionally be revealing of biographical detail. Up until this point, she had only considered confidentiality to be in relation to the client, rather than in relation to both parties in the relationship. This was a moment of re-visioning what the boundary of confidentiality meant. Elizabeth's first response at the thought of recording sessions included a fear of how the recordings might be used, in the event of the therapeutic relationship failing at some point in the future. The re-visioning conversation confirmed that this was an attitude of fear-based practice, and not what she wanted to shape her decision. It was not until Elizabeth explored this with Mary that she realised that what she brought to the session was also bounded by confidentiality. This fact meant that Elizabeth was able to make an authentic decision not to allow the sessions to be recorded, rather than a decision based on fear.

Re-visioning is a seeing something from a different perspective, invariably possible when there is another person present – a supervisor or colleague. In Chapter 5 we will explore other forms of 're-visioning' in the processes of consultation, ethical review and mediation.

The therapeutic relationship

Turning now to the therapeutic relationship, our third cornerstone, it has long been assumed that the quality of this relationship is the core healing agent in therapy (Binder et al, 2009). However, more recent research suggests that the degree to which relationship quality influences therapeutic outcomes may not be as great as was once thought (Cooper, 2010: 188). It now appears that the style of therapeutic intervention – for example, whether or not the therapist provides 'homework' – may itself contribute to the development and strengthening of the relationship. Whatever attitudes the client brings to the relationship, such as the anticipation and appreciation of benefit to themselves, are also significant. Other research suggests that within the relationship itself, it is through moments of relational depth that beneficial change occurs (Knox and Cooper, 2011: 239).

If the theoretical and philosophical framework is the core of the therapeutic model, the relationship is the heart of practice. The style of relationship is largely determined by the therapeutic model. The message is: 'This is how I am going to be in relationship with you'. And 'how I am going to be in relationship with you' involves different dimensions of relationship: personal; interpersonal; transpersonal; and transferential. Each dimension is characterised by relational processes or events. For example, the 'real' relationship or therapeutic alliance is where meeting, contact, interpersonal bonding take place. Or the 'reparative' relationship can help de-toxify and de-intensify a client's experience of previously intolerable emotions of abandonment, rejection, or abuse. The 'transpersonal' dimension is where meaning-making can unfold in relation to 'non-ordinary states of consciousness' (Grof, 2000: 1–19); for instance, spirituality and dreams, as well as an exploration of our relationship with the more-than-human worlds (Abram, 1997, 2010). The 'transferential' dimension enables an exploration of how relationship patterns based on the experience with early care-givers get projected into (either positively or negatively) and re-enacted in the therapeutic relationship.

As illustrated in many of the vignettes of therapeutic situations throughout this book, the transferential dimension of the therapeutic relationship might need particular attention. Client and therapist do appear to 'transfer' into the therapeutic relationship feelings, thoughts, beliefs and attitudes from significant and often unresolved previous experiences. It is arguable that, whatever our core therapeutic approach, due consideration needs to be given to transference and counter-transference. A psychoanalytic or psycho-dynamic therapist will see the potential working through of transference as the basis for successful therapy. This is how the client often brings to consciousness their own unique developmental legacy, and comes to understand its long-term influence. This therapist will be willing to become a 'parental' figure to their client, in order to allow the transference to develop. This enables the client to see the often unhelpful repetition of early relational patterns.

A more person-centred therapist will notice, with their client, if they seem to be relating 'as if' the therapist was the parent or some other authority figure. This therapist would not foster transferential relating, but bring it out into the open for discussion. Similarly, such a therapist needs an ability to spot when they are relating 'as if' they were some figure from the client's past – to know what their own counter-transference response might be.

Whatever our therapeutic approach across this spectrum, we can understand transference and counter-transference phenomena as ways of attempting to be in a relationship. The therapeutic relationship is therefore based *in part* on each partner's unresolved developmental history, as evidenced in transferential relating, and *in part* on the possibilities for relating in the real, current, equally adult collaboration in therapy.

One truth of being human is that the greatest suffering can often be caused by trauma, abuse, betrayal, and abandonment within a relationship. And it is often through a breach of boundary or a methodological mistake in the therapeutic relationship, either perceived or real, that complaints arise, as we shall see in Chapter 5. As therapists, we try to live out our philosophical values in the way we relate to our clients, adjusting ourselves to the ways in which the client changes and grows over the course of a period of therapy. If a problem or conflict emerges between therapist and client, we seek a resolution which holds to our core values.

While some of the greatest challenges to the therapist might well be relational ones, the contemporary therapist is also challenged by new and unfamiliar contexts in which therapy can be practised. These include options as wide-ranging as 'therapy over the internet' and 'therapy in nature'. Therapy is developing in both these directions. Research on the impact of these new contexts for the therapeutic relationship is in its infancy, but there is equal scope here for safe and creative therapy, with the backing of appropriate training and experience.

● ● *Pause for thought: qualities of relating* ● ● ●

- *Divide your notebook page in half vertically. On the left hand side, list those values and principles you identified earlier in 'pause for thought: values underpinning therapy' (p. 27). On the other half of the page, make a list of the personal qualities you think you bring to the therapeutic relationship.*
- *Consider to what extent your personal relational qualities and the values inherent in your therapeutic model are well- or ill-matched. Are there any conflicts or mis-matches? Are there values that seem very significant to your own personal relating style?*
- *Do your personal qualities suggest that other values not so far listed should now be included?*

After working on this exercise during a workshop for trainee therapists, two participants came up with the following responses. Colin considered respect, autonomy, fairness, optimism, and the capacity to enable the reduction of psychological pain and suffering as his core values. These corresponded to a list of qualities which he brought into the therapeutic relationship – acceptance, empathic understanding, sincerity, genuineness, patience, reliability, competence, strength or endurance, fidelity, self-awareness, gentleness, the ability to maintain appropriate boundaries, and trust in the therapeutic process.

Kate considered self-actualisation, respect, compassion, and a belief in self-determination as her core values. These corresponded to relational qualities similar to Colin's but with some important differences – genuineness, tenderness, being an expert on the process of therapy but not on the person's life, boundedness, humility, acceptance, competence, warmth, the ability to hear rather than to simply listen, trustworthiness, competence, responsibility, and the capacity to be empathic.

It is interesting to see from these responses how values seem to constitute a backdrop to the practitioner's way of relating, with the different personal qualities traceable back to a core value. This is undoubtedly an organic, conscious and unconscious process, and values and relational qualities will develop over time, priorities will shift, and new themes emerge.

Methodologies or styles of intervention

Within the therapeutic relationship, therapists' methodologies or interventions are designed to bring about change or ease suffering. This process can usefully be understood with reference to an 'opening-closing' metaphor. Openings are processes which are non-defensive, allowing, expansive, and creative. Closings are processes which are self-protective, narrowing, fixing, defining, and safe. Within this metaphor suffering might be understood as containing aspects of closing or self-protective contraction. For instance, these might include a suspicion or avoidance of opening out to relationships, or perhaps a closing in to fear or sadness in the face of loss or disappointment; whereas openness to the new can bring change and fresh possibilities. Thinking back to our figure of eight, if one area expands then the other area equally contracts.

One of the aims of therapy, it might be argued, is for the client to learn to be more open than closed. While the capacity for opening includes the freedom to choose to close, it is more difficult to choose to be open if the client's default position in life is closed off. This is not to de-value the appropriateness of closing as an important self-protective process, such as in a client's defences. When we sit with and work through these closing process, it is possible for something new and fresh to be brought into the open, as the following vignette demonstrates.

VIGNETTE: 'PETER AND JAMES'

This conversation is taken from a session during the early stages of therapy. Peter, a man in his mid-30s, was finding it particularly difficult to gain a sense of direction in life. Despite graduating with a good degree, he had been employed in a succession of unfulfilling jobs, all of which he had eventually left. At the point of entering therapy he was considering resigning from his present position in marketing to live with his girlfriend in Austria. During this particular point in the session he had came to the realisation that this was not what he wanted.

Peter: [*opening*] It feels as if, yet again, I'm not sure about my direction in life.

James: [*intervention to open*] What is it that prevents you from joining your girlfriend in Austria?

Peter: [*closing*] I'm afraid of making the wrong decision.

James: [*intervention to open*] How might you be able to find out?

Peter: [*opening*] By taking a risk, I guess.

James: [long open silence]

Peter: [*opening*] Perhaps it's that . . . taking a risk.

James: [*intervention to enable further opening*] What are you feeling as you contemplate taking a risk?

Peter: [*closing*] Fear [*pause*] Yeah, fear.

James: [*intervention to enable opening*] It's OK. Try to stay with the fear.

Peter: [*silence followed by opening*] I guess I am afraid of making a mistake again. [*pause*] I know you can't tell me, but what do you think I should do?

James: [*closing feeling of resistance to the question, then opening*] Yes, you're right I can't tell you. [*pause*] Sometimes it's really difficult knowing what to do, and mistakes happen. [*pause*] But perhaps there comes a time when we no longer allow a mistake to prevent us from trying again.

The session continued to explore what 'making a mistake again' might mean. James also helped Peter to surf his feelings more rather than to go into them, thereby enabling him to develop his capacity of opening. Then:

James: [*closing*] I'm aware that we only have a few minutes left, and suggest we pick up next week from where we left off today.

Peter: [*opening*] Yes, that would be good.

In this vignette we see how James enables Peter to be more open to his experience in the present moment rather than remain closed. It is only by opening that Peter gains insight into his issues, and the underlying themes.

   It is likely that frequent experiences of opening rather than closing help us build confidence to face life more fully. There are many ways of enabling opening. Cognitive Behavioural Therapy (CBT), for instance, might enable opening through releasing the client from unhelpful thinking processes. Any modality, methodology or intervention can potentially enable an opening process, but this is also dependent on the therapist's quality of presence – a presence that is not only open but also subject to appropriate boundaries. It is the therapist's responsibility to model this way of being, and it is hoped that through this modelling the client is also able to learn to be open, yet with boundaries. It is both the style of intervention, and the quality of therapeutic presence, then, that enable the client to develop insight and awareness, and consequently to bring about desired change.

The therapist's need for self-care and self-compassion

The relational nature of therapy means that 'if I take care of me I am able to take care of you'. This relates back to one of our core values mentioned earlier: self-respect. However, this cornerstone is the one which therapists often neglect. Self-care has two main dimensions: the self-compassion that is at the heart of our personal self-care, and the professional support that resources our self-care while at work with our clients.

Some of the reasons that could lead us as therapists to neglect our self-care might include the following:

- we feel that if we take a break, this might hinder the therapeutic process, and that the client may regress;
- we will miss the income which the therapy generates;
- we have become unhealthily dependent on the client;
- we feel that a break would create too much negotiation and rescheduling to fit in with our other clients;
- we fear turning down referrals just in case there are no more forthcoming;
- we find it difficult to put ourselves first;
- we are too defined by the role of therapist, to the detriment of other aspects of our identity and life experience; for instance, our relationship with our partner or friends, simply being on our own, or adventuring.

What is evident is that without self-care and self-compassion it is likely that our practice will be in some way be impaired. It seems that self-care and client care are inseparably linked. To neglect one side of the relationship is in a sense to neglect the other, as this creates a relational environment tinged with that neglect. Of course, the client contributes to this too, but it is mostly the therapist's responsibility to repair, and where appropriate to address this. The therapist carries responsibility for their self-care both personally and professionally, as neglect in either area can impact on the therapy.

Fundamental to taking care of oneself is learning to practise self-compassion. Therapists are so familiar with offering compassion to others that they often forget that compassion is not complete unless it is also offered to oneself. The ethic of self-respect goes some way toward addressing this, but self-compassion both includes and goes beyond self-respect. Although the practice of self-compassion is not new, some writers – for example Neff (2011), Germer (2009), Gilbert (2009) – have brought it more fully to our attention. At the heart of self-compassion are the insights that self-kindness is preferable to self-judgement or self-attack, and that mindfulness is preferable to an over-identification or over-association with thoughts and feelings, particularly negative ones. The practice of self-compassion encourages and enhances our well-being. We come to value more the development of a range of emotional states and thinking processes, such as: gentleness; warmth; joy; loving presence; generosity; allowing; letting go; stillness; humility; and discernment. We also learn to trust our own bodily felt wisdom as a guiding factor to what might be necessary in any given situation. Try this next exercise as a way of noticing your own self-compassion.

● ● ● Pause for thought: the practice of self-compassion ● ● ●

- *Begin with bringing your attention to your breathing. Simply notice the rise and fall of your breath until you experience a sense of peace. Focusing our attention on our breathing often has a calming effect.*
- *Bring to mind a concern (past or present) that has been troubling you. Notice your thoughts and feelings in relation to this concern. Try to get a full sense of these.*
- *Then begin to let go of the narrative – the 'story' – associated with this concern, but stay with the felt experience of this. Imagine your concern as a wave passing through you, trusting that a sense of peace or rest will follow. Consider this as moving from closing to opening or fixating to releasing.*
- *Then quietly say to yourself: this also happens, and nothing is permanent.*
- *Then, when you are ready, let this exercise go.*
- *What were your experiences during this exercise? Was there a point where you felt a sense of self-compassion? If so, what was the quality of that feeling?*

The cumulative effects of practising self-compassion include increased self-awareness, as well as a better capacity to discern personal needs and take them into account. Kristin Neff (2011) has also shown how the practice of self-compassion counters a range of negative thinking processes, and is more effective than attempting to develop self-esteem. It is well worth investing time and personal space in developing self-compassion, and some of the books listed under 'Further Reading' at the end of this chapter offer more exercises for you to try.

The professional side of self-care includes continued professional development (CPD), ongoing certified training, therapy, supervision, and sometimes other supports. Our various professional organisations offer advice on the nature and amount of professional self-care considered appropriate. For example, the British Association for Counselling and Psychotherapy (BACP) state that practitioners have a responsibility to themselves to ensure that their work does not become detrimental to their health or well-being. Practitioners are advised to put adequate supportive structures in place to support them in their work (www.bacp.co.uk/ethical_framework/). The 'taking care of me is also taking care of you' maxim of this cornerstone also includes important processes or structures which take care of both parties, such as the appointment of your therapeutic executor, the process of ethical review, and an awareness of your organisation's complaints procedure. These are matters taken up in later chapters.

To end this section, we will look at the ways in which notes and records support therapist self-care, whilst ensuring that the client's therapeutic journey is regularly reviewed. The main purposes of record keeping are to support the therapist and the client in the process of therapy, and assist the therapist in keeping track of the emergence and development of important themes and issues, as well as to inform periodic reviews of the therapy.

● ● ● *Pause for thought: record keeping* ● ● ●

- *What are the different types of notes or records that you use in your practice?*
- *How do you ensure confidentiality? Are you the only person who sees these notes, or do you share them with anybody else? What about the idea of 'professional discretion' in a situation where confidentiality might be held by more than one professional within that setting?*
- *What use do you make of your notes?*

There are many different types of notes and records kept by therapists, and there is a wealth of advice on how to manage this aspect of our practice (some sources are listed in the 'further reading' at the end of this chapter). Perhaps the most important thing is that, as therapists, we each know why we make the records we do, what form they should take and how long we need to keep them. Records might include the contact details of:

- your clients;

- your supervisor;

- your supervisees;

- employee assistance providers and others whom you may be contracted with;

- the settings in which you practice;

- your accrediting and registration bodies;

- your professional liability insurers;

- your therapeutic executor (who may also be the recipient of your records in the event of your incapacity or demise). See Resource 9, Therapeutic Executor Guidelines, below pp. 115–16.

To ensure that you keep records in a safe and legal way, it is worth familiarising yourself with the relevant sections of the Data Protection Act (DPA) which can be found at www.dataprotectionact.org. The third principle (of eight) of the DPA states that records need to be 'adequate, relevant and not excessive'. This needs to be interpreted within the context of your practice. The fourth principle is that records 'need to be accurate and up to date', and the fifth, 'not kept any longer than necessary'. Most insurance companies advise therapists that records are to be kept securely for seven years.

It is perhaps in the use you make of your notes and records that you can be most creative. Take Dennis, for example, a counsellor who works with private clients at home. He has developed a set of records that support him, and these are included in the 'resources' section at the end of this book.

● ● ● Pause for thought: keeping records ● ● ●

Please turn to the 'resources' section, and read the series of record sheets, 1, 2, 3 and 4 (pp. 104–8).

You will see that the first of Dennis's records is a card index summary (Resource 1) which holds the client's contact information and the dates of assessment, contracting and subsequent counselling sessions, all in one place. Because it includes information that identifies the client, this type of record may need to be produced if required by law in the case of any legal investigation. Dennis keeps this information in a secure place and only on cards, not on his computer.

Secondly, Dennis has an 'initial meeting and assessment proforma' record which he compiles after his initial session or sessions with a new client (Resource 2). He uses this as a support when introducing work with a new client to his supervisor. That discussion will often result in a 're-visioning' process that clarifies some of the aims of counselling which can then be discussed with the client, as Dennis and the client make an agreement to work together. (The next chapter will discuss these therapeutic agreements in more detail.) The initial meeting and assessment sheet, plus any subsequent therapeutic agreement, are kept safely by Dennis until the client has finished therapy, and then for seven years after that, as his insurance company advises.

The last kind of notes kept by Dennis are his ongoing session notes (Resource 3). Again, he uses these notes to support his developing reflections on work with a client and finds it useful to take these to supervision sessions as an aide-mémoire. Dennis also finds it helpful, from time to time, to look back over these session notes, in order to gain a picture of how themes or issues are developing and changing over time. Resource 4 gives an example of one of these session notes. As you can see, these ongoing thoughts and ideas contain some mention of Dennis's own process as a therapist, as well as thoughts on the client. Note, however, that the client is not identifiable by name or other personal detail. Dennis keeps these 'process' notes in a special personal journal or folder, so that they are held quite separately from other records in which the client is identifiable. Because these 'process' notes are for his personal use only, Dennis would not show them to anyone else, and he destroys them when they have ceased to be useful. This might be done, for example, after the notes have been used in a supervisory review of this client's work, or if not then, at the end of the therapy period.

As Dennis's notes and records illustrate, we need to be both ethically aware and willing to be creative in finding an appropriate style and content for records for our own use.

Chapter summary

This chapter has encouraged you to reflect on the 'cornerstones' of safe and creative therapeutic practice. You will have given consideration to the balance of creativity and safety in your own practice, and identified key values and principles informing your approach. The chapter also discussed the boundaries of ethics, competency and supervision before exploring the cornerstones of relationship, methodology and style of intervention and, lastly, the therapist's need for self-care and self-compassion. We then considered record-keeping as an important support for a safe therapeutic process.

Further reading

Beebe, J. (2005) *Integrity in Depth*. College Station: Texas A&M University Press. This core value is considered from a range of perspectives, exploring what is meant by integrity and what gets in the way of living it, as well as illustrating how it can inform therapeutic practice.

Bond, T. and Mitchels, B. (2008) *Confidentiality and Record Keeping in Counselling and Psychotherapy*. London: Sage. This practical resource answers many of the questions therapists ask about these two important areas of therapeutic practice.

Lichner Ingram, B. (2011) *Clinical Case Formulations: Matching the Integrative Treatment Plan to the Client* (3rd edn). London: Wiley. This book is a welcome alternative to the diagnostic, often impersonal, labelling of clients, and emphasises the importance of taking the unique need of each client into account when formulating a plan for treatment.

Nhat Hanh, T. (2010) *Reconciliation: Healing the Inner Child*. Berkeley, CA: Parallax Press. This offers meditative reflections and exercises that encourage self-care and self-compassion.

O'Brien, M. and Houston, G. (2004) *Integrative Therapy: A Practitioner's Guide*. London: Sage. Of particular interest in this book is Chapter 7, 'Tools of the Trade', which gives an insightful glimpse into 'being' and 'doing' in therapy.

Sprang, G., Clark, J.J. and Whitt-Woosley, A. (2007) 'Compassion fatigue, compassion satisfaction, and burnout: factors impacting a professional's quality of life', *Journal of Loss and Trauma*, 12 (3): 259–80. This article helps us to understand the importance of self-care and self-compassion.

CHAPTER 3

CREATING AND MAINTAINING THERAPEUTIC AGREEMENTS

Making an initial agreement with your client

Some kind of therapeutic agreement always exists between therapist and client. The agreement might be implicitly recognised by both parties: a tacit agreement. Or it might be more explicit: the expression of therapeutic ground rules, boundaries and expectations. Therapists – perhaps especially those in private practice – have varied opinions about the degree of formality they require of therapeutic agreements.

We are going to argue in this chapter for the value of making and maintaining explicit therapeutic agreements – or 'contracts' – with clients. Tacit agreements often rest on assumptions like 'both of us know what therapy entails'. This may not be the case. Misunderstanding can occur in any therapeutic pairing where one party is 'in the know' about therapy and the other not. For instance, the therapist may think that therapy is concerned with supporting the client's agency and choice, whereas the client might come to therapy looking for help and guidance. Whilst these views are not mutually exclusive, they do express different emphases regarding the aims of therapy. If left unspoken and unchallenged, such differences of understanding can grow into grounds for client dissatisfaction and complaint.

As Charlotte Sills argues, there are some 'powerful advantages' in therapists making clear and explicit contracts. She cites research which shows that such contracts lead more often to successful therapeutic outcomes; provide a yardstick for therapeutic effectiveness; and give more clarity of focus in ongoing therapy (Sills, 2006: 15). Many professional therapist organisations reflect similar views in their ethical frameworks and codes of conduct. The British Association for Counselling and Psychotherapy, for example, expects counsellors to 'engage in explicit contracting in advance of any commitment by the client' (BACP, 2007).

Explicit agreements with clients are valuable in helping to provide a secure framework for ethical and creative practice, in keeping with our 'boundaries cornerstones', discussed in Chapter 2. All the examples used in this chapter are not only explicit, but also *written* therapeutic agreements. Whilst there are no statutory legal reasons why a therapeutic agreement should be in writing, there are strong ethical and professional reasons for this. The content of the written agreement or contract we negotiate with clients reinforces our joint therapeutic intentions and indicates our way of working together. As such, it is less vulnerable to the possibility of conflicting memories, should a complaint arise later on (Bond, 2010: 94).

The process of making a written agreement with a new client also requires care, creativity and empathy. Contracting is indeed a *process* and needs to be given time. Mitchels and Bond remind us that 'clients who are distressed or anxious may not understand clearly all the implications of what they are told in an initial session' (2010: 49). As therapists, we therefore need to develop our skill and understanding in dealing with contracting issues in the process of therapy. Contracting is a significant part of the creative, collaborative work of counselling and psychotherapy, and an important aspect of our developing 'practical wisdom'.

● ● ● *Pause for thought: the basic therapeutic agreement* ● ● ●

- *Make a list of the features that you would include in any explicit agreement you make with a new client.*
- *Why would you include these features, and how would you express them clearly, to new clients?*
- *How might different clients respond to your basic agreement? Might this affect how you proceed with them?*

Your basic therapeutic agreement with a new client will try to reflect or express your cornerstone values, beliefs and practices. It will lay down some clear boundaries about such things as money; times, dates, duration, the regularity of sessions; your availability as therapist; and the limits of confidentiality. It will reflect to some degree your way of working and will set out the expectations of therapist and client. Some readers will use formal, written-down contracts; others will have a list of points for discussion with a new client. Whichever mode you employ, let us call this your 'basic agreement' or 'contract'.

The question about how different clients might respond to a basic agreement, and how this might affect your work with them, is a more complicated matter. To open this up for discussion, we will now look in some detail at the examples of basic written agreements and contracts in the 'resources' section at the end of this book. These examples include a variety of counselling and psychotherapy contracts. Please remember, however, that they are not 'models'. There is no real substitute for creating your own agreement, both in content, style and the way in which you collaborate with your client in creating it. No two clients will respond in exactly the same way to your basic contract. It is worth taking time to discuss the issues and develop a sense of an agreement shared and jointly owned with, rather than imposed on, a new client.

Pause for thought: Resource 5, Contract Example A: ●●● health-centre counselling contract

You will find Contract Example A in the 'resources' section (p. 109). Please now read it through, jotting down any points about it which strike you as interesting or significant.

Let's imagine that this contract is the one being used by Elise, a student counsellor in her practitioner year. She is on a voluntary placement at an NHS health centre. Her clients are sent this 'counselling contract' at the same time as the notification of their first appointment, so they see it before they meet Elise in person. You will have noticed, first of all, that in this contract clients are referred to as 'patients', a term Elise accepts as normal in a GP surgery. However, as you may have said to yourself, there is a possible downside to a term like this in a therapy context. The word 'patient' originally meant 'one who suffers' but has come to mean someone who is 'sick' and in need of medical help. Using this term can reinforce the idea that the therapist will offer a 'cure' rather than work with someone to help them deal with the life issue they are facing. Elise herself does not consider the term 'patient' ideal, but she tries to find the opportunity to explore these perceptions a little during the very first meeting, when she is going over the contract with a new patient.

This contract has very clear boundaries around times and dates, something Elise finds helpful. She notices how different patients react to such a framework. Some are fastidious about arriving and leaving on time and come for all of their six sessions. Others find it hard to comply with these limits for practical reasons such as work or family commitments. Others will express their central therapeutic issue in the way they handle these boundaries. For example, a depressed patient may find it difficult to motivate themselves to travel to the surgery to see a counsellor.

VIGNETTE: 'ELISE AND JEREMY'

Jeremy, one of Elise's 'patients', failed to come to his first session. Following a discussion with her supervisor, it was decided that Elise should try telephoning Jeremy the day before his next session to remind him of their appointment. He was surprised but pleased to hear from Elise, as he had thought that he had 'mucked it up' by not attending the first session. She was able to convey the message that she had been expecting him and been disappointed, but that there were still five sessions left in which they could try to work together to help him deal better with his depression. When he did come for the second session, Elise concentrated on the de-motivating effects of Jeremy's depression and the mistaken view he had held that Elise would not 'miss him' if he did not come. After a somewhat shaky start, he did then make use of all the remaining counselling sessions.

● ● ● **Pause for thought: Resource 6, Contract Example B:** ● ● ●
psychotherapy contract

*We want you now to read through a different agreement, Contract Example B
(pp. 110–11). As you read it, note any features that strike you as significant.*

We'll imagine that this is a contract developed by Brian, a psychotherapist who
has been running a private practice at his own home for 15 years. This contract
is given in written form to each client at the first session, once it has been
established in principle that Brian and the client both wish to work together. At
the same time, he also hands out written information about his professional
organisation's ethical code and complaints procedure. Brian says that, from his
experience, some clients will reply with 'everything is fine' and want to sign the
contract then and there. In a positive sense, this is a clear indication of the client's
eagerness to begin therapy and their initial confidence in the therapist. He
nevertheless considers it important to go through the points carefully to ensure,
as far as possible, a shared understanding. Sometimes this process can be
completed in one or two sessions. Often, a portion of the available time over
several introductory sessions might be devoted to contracting. Brian views this
as time well spent.

Looking at the features listed on this psychotherapy agreement, you will
have noticed that the wording indicates that it is an 'open-ended' contract,
which is not unusual in psychotherapy. It is hard to know right at the outset
how long the process of self-awareness, change and renewal might take for an
individual client, and this needs recognising. But Brian's contract adds,
'which can be reviewed at any time'. It is all too easy for clients to feel that
they have become entrapped in a long-term therapy for the therapist's reasons
not theirs, and this is a relatively common source of complaint against
therapists (Khele et al., 2008: 128). Aside from this safety measure though, the
possibility of review is written into the agreement because of Brian's cornerstone values. It seems necessary to highlight both the 'open-endedness' of the
therapeutic journey and the ongoing joint responsibility of therapist and client to say if they think the therapy might be changing focus or indeed coming
towards an end point.

Brian's contract is also clear about money matters. In private practice and in
some voluntary sector settings, money changes hands. Many therapists feel
uncomfortable with this at quite a deep level. 'It seems like being paid for caring!' as one supervisee put it. Brian feels very differently: his view is that he is
not being paid for 'caring'. No amount of money could ensure that he sincerely
cares for his clients. He is being paid for his time, including the time he has put
into training, continuing professional development and supervision of his practice. He is being paid to ensure that he cares for himself enough to care for others, so he expects to earn a living wage as an independent earner. He is not
being paid for his care, commitment and willingness to be at the service of his

clients in a professionally ethical way. These attributes hopefully come from a genuine, willing and generous place in him; in a sense, he believes they have to be 'freely' given to be real and effective for his clients.

● ● ● Pause for thought: money and fees, value and currency ● ● ●

- *What is your policy, or your organisation's policy, on the handling of the counselling or psychotherapy fee?*
- *What are some of the issues in your experience that have arisen, or that you can imagine arising, with different clients regarding money and fees?*
- *In what ways have you responded, or might you respond, to the issues you have identified?*

Maybe your policy, or your organisation's policy, has some features in common with Brian's. His agreement is succinct about fees. It states how much the client is expected to pay and when they have to pay, and it also informs them that fees will sometimes rise. With such a contract, the new client is clearly entering into a financial arrangement.

Money has meaning for all clients – and therapists. You will have listed a range of issues that might arise. Often the belief that therapy is 'good value' is associated with the client's attitude to money, and to giving and receiving, as much as their ability to pay the fee. In conversations with colleagues and supervisees you might notice responses that reflect their ongoing discomfort about 'paying for caring'. Sometimes a client will ask for a reduced fee, or concession. Even if there are grounds for giving a concession, it seems vital to find out the therapeutic meaning of the client's request – and the therapist's response. The financially poor client, for example, may have real need of a reduced fee but feel demeaned by asking. They might also imagine that the therapist has little need of money, as compared with themselves. Without an open and respectful discussion, such a tangle of assumptions can go unchallenged, only to arise later in the therapy.

You will have your own thoughts on this and your own experiences to share. The values, beliefs and assumptions which underpin your practice will be your own, and will inform how you respond. But we hope you can see that your contract or therapeutic agreement can be a creative expression of your practical wisdom and way of working as a therapist, informing the joint understanding between you and your client. If you look again at Brian's basic contract you will see that as well as clarifying boundaries of time, therapist availability and confidentiality, he also tries to give an indication of other important matters. His philosophy comes through in the care he takes about the 'therapeutic space' (point 5); in his description of the therapeutic relationship (point 10); and in the many references to 'us', 'we' and to being in the therapeutic venture 'together'.

Personalising the therapeutic agreement

Thus far we have been discussing the basic agreement that creates a clear framework for the collaborative and creative enterprise that is therapy. As well as negotiating and agreeing the ground rules, the first contract can also set out the individual focus for therapy as understood by both parties. Making the agreement personal to the individual client can enrich this initial contracting process. The following vignette shows how a client can become involved in the development and revision of a contract.

VIGNETTE: 'ELISE AND AMIR'

Elise, the student counsellor we met earlier in this chapter, was holding her first session with Amir, a client who had previously had six sessions with another counsellor at the health centre. This time his GP had referred him for a longer period of 24 counselling sessions. Amir told Elise that he had returned to counselling because 'they all think I should get some more help'. His wife had told him he was no help to her and the children, even though he 'had no job and plenty of spare time'. He felt 'useless because she's so much better with the kids than me'. He had been employed to do some temporary work with a local firm but had recently been laid off again following an altercation with his manager. He complained that he was 'so fed up with feeling like I'm bad'. Elise asked him to experiment with saying those words in different ways, with different voices. When he did so, Amir first discovered a deep sadness at the heart of his words. As he repeated the words, however, he went on to feel frustrated, puzzled, then annoyed and finally indignant. During this exercise he became more aware of the range of feelings he himself was experiencing and his excitement and energy visibly increased. Following this work, Elise and Amir added a 'thing I want to change' to his standard counselling contract. This reflected Amir's new understanding that he often stored up his feelings, relying on others to tell him how he felt. He wanted to become more able to communicate his own feelings. Amir now understood that other people might be 'helped' as a spontaneous effect of his own work in therapy but his primary aim was to do his own work.

● ● ● *Pause for thought: Resource 7, Contract Example C:* ● ● ●
Hillside Therapy Centre: client agreement

Please now turn to the Resources section again, and read Example Contract C (p. 112). We will imagine that this is the basic contract used by Rob. He trained as a counsellor 15 years ago and, following further training, now works as a therapist specialising in trauma work at a private group practice. The group centre's standard agreement is for open-ended therapy, offered to clients who may often be self-referred. Once again, please make notes on anything in this contract that strikes you as significant.

The process of making and personalising an agreement can raise complex therapeutic issues. To explore some of these, the following vignette and 'pause for thought' show how Rob makes this agreement specific to an individual client.

VIGNETTE: 'ROB AND CLAIRE'

Rob has had an initial session with a new client, Claire, who was at first rather vague about her reasons for seeking therapy. Although she had worked with several previous therapists, she seemed relatively un-self-aware. When relating her childhood story of repeated and violent assault, she showed signs of dissociation in her level, vacant gaze whilst talking in a rather expressionless way of her experiences. She seemed to lose herself in her story, then jerk back to the reality of the here-and-now, in the therapy room with Rob. She expressed very angry feelings at times but through a fixed smile and clenched jaw. Rob wondered if re-telling her story to a series of previous therapists had done little more than cause Claire to re-live, rather than integrate and resolve, her issues from childhood. He noted that she had trusted him enough – or been desperate enough – to provide a lot of detail at this first session. In transferential terms, such trust might express her need for a 'safe adult' to take care of her 'abused child'.

Rob felt very protective of her but also a bit wary. He recognised these feelings as his familiar counter-transference response to such clients. He did not openly share his thoughts with Claire but held them as information for himself, to be discussed with a colleague if necessary. Whilst Claire wanted intimacy with a safe adult, judging by all her attempts at therapy, she might also be terrified of close emotional contact with a therapist she did not, as yet, know well enough to trust in a grounded way.

● ● *Pause for thought: contracting therapeutic boundaries* ● ● ●

- *How would you advise Rob to make use of the contracting process in the circumstances described in this example?*
- *How might Rob personalise this client's therapeutic agreement in a way that might benefit the therapy without compromising good boundaries?*
- *Now read the remainder of the vignette, and compare your own responses with what Rob actually did.*

Rob suggested that he and Claire make an agreement together, beginning with the clear boundaries laid down by the centre's contract. Instead of starting with an open-ended contract, though, perhaps they should begin in a gentle way which would acknowledge the distress Claire was experiencing. How about meeting once a fortnight for six sessions to see how she found the process of working with Rob? Claire agreed to consider this before the second session. She began the session in a rather irritable and annoyed state, saying she was entitled to open-ended therapy. Rob agreed that she was indeed entitled to help and he could see why she was annoyed. But maybe the distressed child part of her might be less confident? Sometimes, he said, we can be 'in two minds' about something. He had been thinking himself that on the one hand she was an experienced client, so why not? On the other, he could see that she was still affected by the awful experiences she had suffered. With a slower start, she would have more space to get to know Rob and really see if she felt safe 'all through' about working with him.

Claire was moved by Rob's attempt to meet her and understand her mixed feelings. They negotiated an initial contract of 12 weekly sessions, checking in with each other during that time to discuss how things were going. Rob said he was glad of this as otherwise the sessions might easily have got 'filled with content' from Claire's rather fraught life. As it was, this long mutual assessment period did lead on to an open-ended therapy experience for her, and one that was much more grounded and effective than her previous experiences.

Re-contracting: the review and renewal of agreements

Peter Jenkins reminds us that the therapist's duty of care includes 'the use of informed consent, therapeutic contracting and review with clients'(2007: 99). Making a therapeutic agreement, or contract, is not just an initial event; it is also an ongoing process in therapy. It therefore seems important to include opportunities for the client to review the course of their therapy. These opportunities for review can support a shift into a new phase of work and relationship. We can call such a shift 're-contracting', because it is a process by which the original contract is reviewed, modified if necessary, and renewed (Owens, 2007a: 42). Content that may by then have been completed through earlier work is celebrated and explicitly incorporated or put aside, so that client and therapist can give attention to new areas of joint endeavour. We can see how this works in the two vignettes which follow. The first one shows the process of a therapeutic review being suggested by the client.

VIGNETTE: 'JAMAL AND JANICE'
Jamal had been working with Janice for about six weeks when he said 'I want to try to write down something about what I've learned so far in counselling'. He had set out with the aim of working through a long-ago bereavement and in the process uncovered some painful childhood experiences. He had used writing as part of this process, telling the story of his childhood in which the death of his mother was only the beginning. Now he was at a point where he could see the link between, as a child, 'living in dread' of arousing his stepmother's anger, and his current obsessive, phobic thoughts as an adult.

Janice conducted a review with Jamal over several counselling sessions. They talked, then every so often paused whilst Jamal wrote down what seemed significant to him. This was a rewarding, extended dialogue and marked a new phase in their working relationship. Jamal now trusted Janice to help him without taking over his thoughts and feelings, which was something he had experienced in other significant relationships. They decided to record his insights and their ensuing discussion as part of a renewed agreement.

In the second vignette, the process of therapeutic review arises out of a Gestalt 'experiment'. This term denotes a situation where the need arises to challenge something in the client or in the therapeutic relationship. Instead of 'just talking', the therapist suggests an imaginative activity, grounded in their knowledge of the client's self process gained over time, which is designed to engage that client in a more meaningful way. They then support them to use the experiment to change some habitual mode of belief, feeling or action. As Joseph Zinker puts it, an experiment will 'ask the client to express something behaviourally, rather than to merely cognize an experience internally' (1978: 124).

VIGNETTE: 'HENRY AND ANDREW'

Henry had been working for two years with his psychotherapist, Andrew. He felt very preoccupied about his relationship with Murray, his partner of 18 years, having recently discovered that Murray had been having an affair with a much younger man. Though Henry was at first devastated, he and Murray had decided to try and save their relationship. Together, they had gone through a very painful period of trying to rebuild love and trust following this crisis. Henry found that he 'could not take one step forward without being stopped in his tracks by memories of Murray's betrayal'.

Andrew agreed that 'all this talking hadn't helped much'. Instead he suggested an experiment to try 'taking some steps' across the therapy room. Andrew stood beside Henry as he tried to take the first step, which was a tiny but difficult one. Andrew followed, allowing himself to feel the smallness of that step and how hard it was to take. When Andrew verbally shared this experience, Henry felt understood in his pain and difficulty. He also felt able to take another step, and another, across the room. Andrew continued to follow in Henry's steps, sharing his experience with each step. They lost sight of the original connection with Henry's troubled partnership. The focus shifted to the empathic connection between Henry and Andrew, Andrew and Henry.

In the de-briefing conversation afterwards, Henry reflected on the trust, safety and understanding he had experienced with his therapist. Andrew reminded him that this trust and empathy had been earned in the time and energy they had both committed to the relationship; something to celebrate. He also wondered if this was similar to the loving trust that now felt broken between him and his partner. They needed time to put new energy and commitment into their relationship, even though Henry might only take one small step at a time.

Whereas the first vignette showed how a more formal review can occur at an appropriate point in a client's experience of counselling, the second illustrates how a review might emerge more informally in the ordinary course of psycho-therapy. In both examples the therapist employs skill and sensitivity in renewing the contractual understanding shared with their client and re-energising support for the continuing therapeutic journey. The boundaries of the therapeutic work are renewed even as they change and as these developments are registered between them formally or informally.

There will be times, however, when something unexpected can cause us to reconsider contractual boundaries. In such circumstances, how are we to know if a temptation to 'bend the rules' or 'do something different with this client' should indeed be followed by action?

● ● ● **Pause for thought: when therapeutic** ● ● ●
boundaries are challenged

- *Think of a time when something unexpected has emerged in your work with a client. Has a client ever challenged your agreed ground rules in some way? Have you ever been tempted to 'bend the rules' for them?*
- *What happened and what was the effect of this on you and on your client?*
- *How did you (or how could you) have worked through this experience, partially or fully? What might support you in going through such a process?*

Sometimes an unexpected occurrence can take us by surprise, as we see in the following account.

VIGNETTE: 'ANDREA AND MARK'

Andrea was a counsellor on an Employee Assistance Programme (EAP) and used the standard company contract with clients similar to Contract Example D, Resource 8 (pp. 113–14). She was seeing Mark because he had received feedback that his relationships with fellow employees at work were 'inappropriate' and could be 'destructive'.

In the first two sessions, Andrea had learned that Mark came from a large, talkative working-class family and found his 'tight-lipped' colleagues at work hard going. They seemed, he said, not to be able to take a joke and he never knew what they were really thinking. He had been shocked to get a counselling referral but he did nevertheless enjoy his sessions with Andrea 'chewing the cud together'. She was sometimes amused by Mark but at other times found his personal remarks and questions a bit intrusive. She put this down in part to his inexperience of counselling but could see that it might also be at the root of his problems at work. Then, during the third session, Mark whipped out his mobile phone and started turning it around to make video images of the counselling room. Andrea was completely dumbstruck at first. Then she wondered briefly if she should gloss over the incident, as Mark clearly did not see anything wrong in what he was doing. But then her professional self took over. 'Turn your phone off, now, Mark – and I mean right now this instant!' Sheepishly, he turned off his phone. In the discussion which followed, Andrea reminded him that their counselling agreement spoke of the 'confidentiality of this counselling space and what took place there'.

After the session Andrea still felt a bit shocked and, to her surprise, also ashamed. How could she have let this happen? When she took her experience to her own therapy, she shared her feelings of exposure and shame, uncovering some of her 'self-critical perfectionist' values in the process. Then in supervision she reviewed her way of discussing the client contract. She agreed that in future she would spend more time making sure inexperienced counselling clients understood the significance of themes like confidentiality. In later sessions it emerged that Mark had no real understanding of what this meant even though he had 'agreed' to the clause in the contract. Andrea went on to explore Mark's experience of 'not realising', both here and in his work situation where colleagues expected him to keep some things private.

As this vignette illustrates, most examples of challenges to contractual boundaries arise out of the everyday situations of therapy. A client arrives late for a session and you find yourself ending later than the agreed time. Your contract says a client will pay for unplanned missed sessions but when it comes to it, you do not ask them to pay. It is always worth examining what motivates our responses to such situations. Going over an agreed time boundary in such circumstances may seem kind but is also worrying to a client who may need to feel securely contained. We might avoid pressing payment as a way of avoiding an angry response from our client, which could result in their leaving therapy with a consequent loss of income for the therapist. Such issues are useful to take to supervision or to peer discussion. This will support you in maintaining contractual boundaries unless and until there is good reason to change them.

Ending a therapeutic agreement

As we have seen, a clear agreement at the outset of therapy is only a beginning. Your contract needs to be maintained, reviewed and sometimes re-defined as an integral part of the process of therapy. Opportunities for review, including acknowledgement and celebration, as well as the exploration of any areas of concern, may be especially important when a period of therapy is coming to an end. Our practical wisdom as therapists will be just as necessary at the end, as at any other stage of the therapy.

Therapeutic endings can have deep meaning for both client and therapist. This is perhaps why Peter Jenkins includes the 'use of properly negotiated endings for therapeutic contact' in his 'guidelines for professional practice' (2007: 99). Endings are often associated with the other experienced loss or lack of human relationship, and with profound issues of life, death and mortality. Because of this we will each have attitudes, beliefs and personal styles associated with ending. A therapist who has awareness of their own self-process around endings is probably more likely to be able to support their client's ending process.

In one sense, the end of a period of counselling or psychotherapy is written into its beginning. In short-term work the time span is usually specified in the initial contract, as in Contract Example A. This known time frame helps shape the process of counselling. Often the work will begin with introductory and exploratory work, followed by consolidation and development within the time allowed. The concluding phase then provides an opportunity to survey what has been learned and support the client in taking their new awareness with them out into the world. In longer-term work too, as Contract Example B illustrates, the possibilities for ending can be highlighted at the outset. Clause 11 in this contract gives an indication of psychotherapist Brian's preferences for ending therapy with care and collaboration, making it a 'mutual experience'. It shows his openness about how the therapy might end, allowing for a more sudden ending as well as a staged process over time. The intention, he states, is to 'make a good ending for you' as a result of discussion and negotiated decision making.

● ● ● *Pause for thought: different kinds of 'ending'* ● ● ●

- *In your opinion, what is it that makes for a satisfactory ending with a client? Draw on your own experience in noting the things you value at a time of ending.*
- *Consider the range of ways in which a therapeutic ending might prove difficult. Make a note of possible reasons: external to the therapy; within the therapeutic relationship; factors affecting you or the client as individuals.*

In answer to the first question you might agree with workshop participants who thought that a satisfactory ending is one where some or all of the following are found:

- There is a sense of 'job done', at least for now, and a need to acknowledge and appreciate positive gains for the client.

- The client feels ready to make the transition back to living without therapy and the therapist. Usually this entails for the client an experience of supported (not anxious) excitement, in the knowledge that they have changed life patterns or coping mechanisms enough to proceed now without therapy. For some clients, it is helpful to feel that they can return to therapy if necessary at some future point in their lives.

- The therapist also feels ready to let them go in the knowledge that hopefully they have been nourished by the experience and now need to move on. This often means that the therapist must take responsibility for their own sense of loss, not weighing the client down with feelings that do not belong to them.

For these things to happen, we must seek a full experience of ending, with enough time and commitment to explore feelings and thoughts satisfactorily. It is likely that a long-term period of psychotherapy will require a more extended period of appraisal, preparation and completion than a short series of focused counselling sessions. Each ending is, nevertheless, different and such global assumptions are often challenged. A counselling client may have rapidly formed a strong attachment to their counsellor, perhaps as the first person who has recognised their pain. For that client – and, very likely, for their counsellor – the loss will be keenly felt. On the other hand, a psychotherapy client with little empathy or need for relationship may have worked for years with a psychotherapist without seeing them as a complete person. In such circumstances, there might be little evidence of the possible significance of ending therapy for the client. The therapist here would need to deal with their own feelings about such an 'empty' ending.

Susie Lendrum writes that:

> the encounter with the reality of an ending can make this phase particularly powerful and effective in terms of enabling change. Both parties are changed by the experience, and the internalisation of a reflective and more emotionally sensitive relationship can lead to a mutually rewarding ending. (Lendrum, 2004: 35)

Few endings, however, are completely satisfactory and none are perfect. Not all loose ends will be tied, or issues satisfactorily resolved. Sometimes it seems our clients regress, or return to earlier issues we thought had been resolved. Supervision can help us as therapists to process these matters so that we can recognise a good *enough* ending and move on ourselves.

Let us turn now to the second question you considered in the 'pause for thought': about the things that might make an ending difficult. Maybe you have experience of some of these matters. There may be practical reasons for the client ending therapy sooner than expected, such as a house or job move, childcare responsibilities emerging or changing, or financial hardship. Often, the best a therapist can do is support the client's expression of mixed feelings. For example, they may feel excitement about the new job *and* feel dismayed about losing their therapeutic support. Or they might be worried about the expense of therapy and accepting of the need to stop but *also* feel relief at 'having to' leave therapy. The meaning of ending, as in the co-constructed meanings generated by the therapy process as a whole, is easily distorted or split if the therapist fails to make room for the whole story.

Sometimes the client may have an unspoken wish to end the therapy. Maybe they have not experienced enough 'fit' between themselves and their therapist, but felt unable to say so or unheard when they tried. Or it might be that a client detects that their therapist depends on them in some way, and feels unable to 'displease' the therapist by leaving. It is true that for therapists in private practice, at least, losing a client means losing income. For organisations whose funding requires evidence of sustained and 'positive outcomes', losing too many clients is bad news. And for trainee therapists seeking to accumulate enough practice hours, the issue is similar. In such circumstances, we have a responsibility to separate our professional marketing or organisational concerns from the needs of the client who may be ready to go.

More insidiously, therapists in some cases can come to depend on their clients in an emotional way, perhaps enjoying their clients' perceived (but possibly projected) vulnerability or dependence. We need to develop our practical wisdom in noticing when a client might be thinking of leaving, but not saying directly. For instance, a formerly 'child-like' client who starts to 'parent' their therapist might thus be indicating their own readiness to take care of themselves. A client who requests less frequent sessions may be ambivalent about ending but want to try out longer separations. The therapist who notices such things can attend to them with their client and help them to work towards an end, if appropriate.

Other factors that can make it difficult for a client to continue and perhaps lead to a sudden or unexpected ending are found in the relationship, most especially in the tranferential, or 'as if' dimension. This is a point taken up in an interesting way by Joy Schaverien in discussing 'men who leave too soon', where she argues that, sometimes, for a man working with a female therapist, 'intimacy may be feared as threatening their masculinity and drawing them back into the maternal realm'. She also thinks that female therapists are more inclined to conflate the maternal and sexual elements in the counter-transference, making them less likely to deal appropriately with the erotic. In keeping with the psychoanalytic understanding of sexual development, she notes that 'erotic playback between the child and the parent of the opposite sex is essential for a healthy sense of sexual viability', and a male client will often reach a point where he needs to be seen as a sexual being by his transferential 'mother', his female therapist (Schaverien, 1997: 5, 9). This is not, as many female therapists might interpret it, an experience to be viewed solely in the realm of adult sexuality. It is also, crucially, connected to developmental needs to be loved and admired as a male being by a 'mother' who will not abuse her power but will reserve her active sexual desires for her adult partner, not act them out with her 'son'. Confusion, anxiety and misapprehension about these issues arising from erotic transference are, Schaverien argues, one reason why men in therapy with female therapists can sometimes 'leave too soon'.

At other times, endings are difficult because they are unplanned, as is the case with a sudden onset of illness or the death of client or therapist. Even in more satisfactory ending situations, as therapists we deal with adjustment and loss. But a client's sudden illness or death can leave us shaken and sometimes bereaved in a way that is not easy to share, except in our own therapy and supervision. We also need to consider the reverse, when therapy ends due to therapist illness or death. It is important to know that should such unexpected circumstances occur, our clients will be cared for appropriately. If we are working in an organisation we need to know what the policy is, and try to ensure that accurate and up-to-date information on our client work is available to the appropriate channels. In private practice, it is important to make a reciprocal relationship with another therapist to act as therapeutic executor for each other's practice. Most professional organisations offer advice on setting up a 'therapeutic executor' arrangement. One such example, from UKAHPP's advice to members, is reprinted in Resource 9, Therapeutic Executor Guidelines (see pp. 115–16).

Whatever steps we take to support the probability of a satisfactory ending with each of our clients, there is another sense in which therapeutic endings remain unspecified, of necessity. Our cornerstone values require us to respond as best we can to the unique human person who is our client. Practical wisdom supports us to hold the mix of complete and incomplete; the necessarily imperfect ending. The end of therapy will be utterly individual; we must work creatively and responsively to make a 'good ending' for that person. Here each ending is truly an experience that develops out of the process of therapy.

Pause for thought: reflecting on 'endings' ● ● ●

- Consider a therapy 'ending' that you have experienced. In what ways did this experience reflect elements of your therapeutic agreement? Think for example about when it happened and how the ending was conducted.
- How did the 'ending' express your appreciation of this client as a unique individual person?
- To what extent would you say this was a 'good ending' for your client? And to what extent for you? Why was this so?
- Can you identify some key issues that seem to arise at times of ending?

This 'pause for thought' will have encouraged you to reflect on the complexity and variety of therapeutic endings. Maybe you thought of a client who was hard for you to finish with. Perhaps the one who came to mind was the client you could not wait to see the back of. Or maybe you recalled an ending that was moving, even beautiful. Or it is possible you remembered a client whose way of ending was to withdraw, rather than engage with you at that point.

Here is another story from therapy to compare with your own thoughts and memories.

VIGNETTE: 'JO AND GLADYS'

Jo works for a bereavement counselling service. She had an open-ended counselling contract to work with Gladys, a 79-year-old client who had recently lost her husband after 50 years of marriage. In dealing with her sadness and loss over her husband's death Gladys realised that she also needed to look at earlier losses. She had been a sickly child and all her life had felt 'disabled' by severe asthma. She came to recognise the opportunities she might have lost as a result of a lifetime of illness, and Jo supported her in practical steps to improve her health and well-being. Things were going well, when Gladys began to have recurring bouts of illness that effectively made her incapable of attending counselling sessions. Although they both recognised that good work had been completed and if Gladys stopped counselling immediately this benefit would remain, Jo was concerned about Gladys. Having dealt with so much loss in her life previously, an unplanned ending at this point might leave Gladys with another loss to process alone. In discussion with her and with support from her supervision group, Jo negotiated a revised contract to make provision for holding sessions at Gladys's home. They felt that this was a creative solution to a real-life problem. The counselling continued until Gladys thought she had done enough.

When it came, eventually, to the final session, Gladys said their revised arrangement had helped her to accept her illness 'but not in a passive way'. This was something for Jo and Gladys to celebrate. In this last session they also touched on the end of their working relationship. Gladys said that she felt thankful and confident to face the last part of her life. Her relationship with Jo 'would not be lost but carried inside her'. She also shared with Jo for the first time her spiritual understanding that she was being 'held by universal Nature in the cycle of life, death and rebirth'. Jo pondered this after the session and wondered why they had not really talked of such matters before.

Let us consider the 'pause for thought' questions as they relate to this vignette. First, this ending did express Jo's initial commitment to Gladys, even though they had reviewed matters after her repeated illness. In saying that the work had helped her to deal actively with her illness, Gladys was celebrating the achievement of a major goal of counselling identified at the outset: support for her to grow out of the 'passive' habits learnt as a 'sickly child'.

In answer to the second question, 'ending' was a large overall theme in Gladys's therapeutic work. At any point, she could have become too ill to continue counselling or could indeed have died. Jo said that this did, perhaps paradoxically, give Gladys a surer sense of what she wanted to focus on in sessions and helped them to make decisions with an edge of clarity and firmness.

On balance, Jo judged this a 'good enough ending' for Gladys. There was a sense of completion around core areas of Gladys's life work. Jo also felt that the therapeutic relationship had been honoured throughout and reflected in the end of their work together. Even so, the spiritual or transpersonal dimension of Gladys's work could perhaps have been better supported in her counselling exploration. The end of therapy might have afforded a way of developing this dimension, maybe through meditation, prayer, or simply reconnecting with the natural world.

From your own experience, you will have identified key issues that seem to arise at the end of a period of therapy. For now, let us look at three such key issues and relate them to the vignette we have been discussing. First, as Petruska Clarkson points out (1995: 133), both therapist and client will have 'their own preferences for ending'; or if you like, an ending style associated with emotional responses and habits of behaviour learned over their lifetimes. Some of us will typically want to end 'too soon' as a way of not entering into the meaning of ending. Gladys might have accepted her loss of counselling quite readily because she was used to illness causing the disruption and severance of relationship. Others among us will be more prone to dragging out a closing experience, being unwilling to let go of a relationship. Both pre-empting and lengthening the ending process can be a way of avoiding the pain of separation. As therapists we are called to bear this pain, which can sometimes contain all the emotions of the grieving process, as we say goodbye to clients. This is an area where the 'cornerstone' of therapist self-support and self-compassion is of key importance.

The second issue concerns the fact that endings, like all human experiences, are mixed. Some aspects are to be celebrated: the client's personal achievements can be recognised and generalised, supporting them to take their therapeutic 'goodies' out into their lives, work and relationships. Gladys now enjoys her new attitude to a life-long struggle with illness. She values the practical ways she has learnt to support herself better at this late stage in her life. The other side of this coin is loss. Gladys is unlikely ever to see Jo again. This is a parting of the ways. Perhaps because Gladys is coming towards the end of her life, the end of therapy sees her sharing her experience of being 'held' by a sense of the universal. She does not feel she will 'lose' Jo even if she never sees her again.

A third issue arises out of a natural-seeming element in farewells. In their preparation for ending, Jo and Gladys might have discussed 'goodbye gifts' as are given in other situations like a colleague leaving work, or someone going to live a long way away. But Jo would be aware that normal gifts were not just 'normal' in a therapy situation and rarely expressed the meanings intended with much accuracy. She might suggest, instead, that they each write a postcard for the other and bring it to the last session. This could perhaps express more creatively and ethically something of the meaning of 'goodbye' for each of them.

Endings are usually imperfect. The sense of things left unsaid or undone seems inevitable when we think of therapy as an aspect of a lifetime journey for our clients. Yet our responsibility to remain each client's therapist, and hold to our therapeutic agreement, continues right to the end, and even beyond.

Chapter summary

This chapter has highlighted the reasons for making an explicit therapeutic agreement or written contract at the outset of therapy with a new client, arguing for a personalised and negotiated agreement wherever possible. Such agreements need to be maintained and reviewed where necessary as part of an ethical and creative process. When it comes to the end of a period of therapy, whether in short- or long-term work, we need practical wisdom in considering issues that arise for our clients and ourselves. Therapeutic agreements can support the work through to completion.

Further reading

Fox, S. (2008) *Relating to Clients: The Therapeutic Relationship for Complementary Thera-pists.* London and Philadelphia: Jessica Kingsley. The whole book is of use but see, in particular, Chapter 3 on 'Boundaries' which includes an investigation of the contracting process, and Chapter 7 on 'Sex and the Erotic in the Therapeutic Relationship'.

Mitchels, B. and Bond. T. (2010) *Essential Law for Counsellors and Psychotherapists.* London: BACP and Sage. This offers a readable and informative account of the legal and ethical framework of therapy. Chapter 4, 'Contracts', is particularly relevant for this chapter.

Proctor, B. (2002) *The Dynamics of Power in Counselling and Psychotherapy: Ethics, Politics and Practice.* Ross-on-Wye: PCCS Books. Particularly helpful for therapists whose values eschew 'power over' clients, this is an unflinching investigation into the ways we may use power, consciously and unconsciously.

Sills, C. (ed.) (2006) *Contracts in Counselling and Psychotherapy.* London: Sage. This is a collection of detailed discussion papers on the therapeutic contracting process, explored by a range of writers with different professional perspectives.

CHAPTER 4

FRAMING THE THERAPEUTIC PROCESS

An aesthetics of therapy: the language of frames

As we have been discussing in previous chapters, effective therapy requires a considered balance between creativity and safety. While these concepts are not necessarily mutually exclusive, there is often a tension between them. There is, perhaps, a similar tension between the science and the art of therapy. Science tends to prioritise the objective and art tends to prioritise the subjective. Both, however, use hypotheses or 'frames' for exploring things from a particular viewpoint. We might argue that what binds art and science together is the creativity of enquiry. Therapy, in this sense, is a scientific *and* artistic enquiry into the nature of being one's unique self, through the process of meaning-making. As we suggested in Chapter 2, the therapist draws upon a range of evidence-based methodologies, together with more subjective, spontaneous, and intuitive interventions. Like artists, who enable us to see the world differently, the therapist's role is to create the conditions where the client can step outside social convention: to stop, look, listen, experience differently; to play, explore, and ask 'what if' questions about him- or herself.

Therapy, like art, is both an expression and a witnessing. As therapists, we are framing a space for the conscious expression and witnessing of a co-created outcome. We step through and behind social niceties, reach beyond 'I'm fine, how are you'. We engage in a peculiar intimacy, often reported as more significant than other intimate relationships. Therapy can only begin to flow creatively once we have the conditions for genuine intimacy to develop: space, time, no interruptions, deep respect for another, and an earned trust.

When we embark on any creative activity there is nearly always a frame of some sort which contains, enables and supports the process. What is framed is the field of scientific enquiry *and* our space for playful, artistic expression. While both art and science as disciplines try to start with a 'blank canvas', they also engage with the reality of limitations. The emerging 'shape' or 'image' of an artwork might be framed by the dimensions of a space. Think, perhaps, of an installation in a room, or the edge of a canvas. We might refer to this as the environmental frame.

In other art forms like poetry and music, the work is usually framed by time, duration or pacing: think of the metre of a poem or the rhythm of a song. As therapists, we also make creative choices within the limits afforded by time.

Think of the rhythm or beginning and ending of sessions, the therapeutic hour, the extent of therapy over weeks, months or even years.

As we saw in Chapter 3, therapy as a creative activity is also framed by a contract or agreement: the contractual frame. And, as discussed in Chapter 2, the meaning-making theoretical model of the therapist is also a framing system. Within these frames is the relational frame which is co-created with the client. Before considering these matters in more depth it is perhaps worth pausing to reflect further on the significance of frames.

● ● ● *Pause for thought: frames of containment* ● ● ●

- *Thinking of the idea that 'frames hold that which sits within them', take some time to imagine an ideal building and location where you might site your therapy space. Shape it, and put whatever you desire into it, to enable it to provide conditions that will be ideal for you to work with your clients.*
- *Take yourself into the room you have imagined. What would it be like to be 'held' within the frame of this ideal consulting room? If it is helpful, you might take a piece of paper and some drawing materials and make an image to represent this experience.*
- *Then reflect on the real-life limitations of your practice. To help you do this, stand at the threshold of the door of your actual consulting room. Play with moving through the threshold and back again, opening the door, and closing it behind you. Allow yourself to bring your awareness into your body so that you get a felt sense of knowing what it feels like to be held within the frame of your consulting room.*
- *Compare your 'ideal' therapy space with your 'actual' one. How much of your practice is framed in the way you would wish it to be?*

Passing through the frame of the door into your consulting room is an entering into of the space that you have dedicated to the purpose of therapy. The 'rules' are that this space is not to be intruded upon by, for instance, excessive noise or other interruptions. Quite often it is the ambience of the familiar and constant framed space that creates a feeling of safety; where defences can be relaxed or let go of. This atmosphere is underpinned by the frame of the therapeutic contract or mutual agreement. These two frames 'hold' both persons in the room.

The therapist provides the side of the relational frame which holds the process of the work. This frame equates to a situation of safety, of containing maternal attention where the child can relax into the dreamlike 'as if' world of play (Winnicott, 1971: 48, 118). In such a space we can let go, knowing someone else is looking out for real dangers: the car, the alligators, or missing tea time. 'Play' for both child and client is a situation where one's endeavour will be intent and serious, but needs to have no direct impact on real life; it is like a pretend game where one can experiment with ways of being. It is important for the validity of play that we stick to certain 'rules', even if outsiders may not understand their value in preserving the meaning of the game. The parent or therapist has to hold the frame of this 'as if' space, to protect the child/client for a while, from real-life demands. This chapter develops the idea that frames are boundaries which hold and enable the therapeutic process.

The environmental frame

Perhaps the obvious starting point in therapy is that it takes place within a setting (usually a room) in a context such as a private house, the premises of an agency or a college. What is sometimes less obvious is that the context is able to offer a degree of anonymity to the client, and that the setting is strictly private. The key here is being able to set the right environmental conditions for safe and creative work. Whether we practise alone or as part of an organisation will affect how we see ourselves, and how we are seen, and what permissions we can give ourselves to work freely. For example, in one organisation, going out for a walk with an agoraphobic client to try 'loosening their fear' would have invalidated the insurance of the practice.

An approachable building and a well-equipped, spacious enough room with quiet conditions are things it would be good to be able to take for granted. Both parties need to feel relaxed, and undisturbed. In an institutional setting it may be important for therapists to state these needs explicitly, to set the frame. Our ability to show care can be limited by external forces. Therapists working in a community-based service might have room bookings changed unexpectedly. A health or college service might see therapy as a consultation similar to other advice or clinic appointments, and may even expect hot-desking, which cuts across providing environmental constancy. Some managers (with or without any therapy training) will need all this information about the nature of confidentiality and therapeutic space presented as a clinical issue. The clearer we can be in our minds about the values underpinning our therapy, the easier it will be to describe to others the physical conditions we need. When whole departments are moved to inappropriate or inaccessible sites, the therapists involved might feel unsettled and homeless themselves. A lack of value and care for the service provided becomes the underlying theme, and can be projected onto the session. The therapist, too, needs their own boundary and space to feel welcome and sufficiently secure.

For the client, time taken to discuss feelings around the setting and context at the beginning of a contract could be well spent. One client might feel safer, another more intimidated, coming into an institutional context. The space itself is the holding environment for many clients, and change can echo the disruptions of childhood, and beyond. Clients with a more secure attachment style may be genuinely unconcerned, but for others, an apparent lack of concern about changes will signal a retreat to guard themselves from further intimacy.

The person with insecure attachment might say 'I am used to this, it's OK', and then retreat from engagement. At one centre, the arrival of a noisy and boisterous adolescent service on the floor below proved very disturbing for some counsellors and their clients. Others absorbed the noise as 'normal', or even reassuring.

We are perhaps all familiar with the notion of 'transitional objects' which 'function as representatives of the absent mother, permitting the negotiation of separation and the illusion of control' (Abrams and Neubauer, 1978: 140). The vignette below illustrates their use in a difficult therapeutic situation.

VIGNETTE: 'AMY AND DAVID'

Amy was a client of David's at the social and community services centre where he was based as a therapist. She had been with him for a few years, in supportive and reparative therapy. Her life had been one of a long string of changes: a sudden collapse of her original family, a move to a children's home, foster care, school moves, and, once into adult independence, a traumatic move from a violent partner. It was a vulnerable time for her and her children. Her attachment to the peaceful therapy/play therapy room had become important. Suddenly, the whole unit was due to move and David with it too, with one month's notice. Amy felt unexpectedly shaken up, with fears that David, like her real father, would use the move to disappear. This was a valuable but risky time in the therapy. Addressing the pragmatic, adult level, she went along with her social worker to the new site, to check out the journey. Then, attending to the terrified child within Amy, she and David spent a session choosing something to act as a talisman, a 'transitional object' that would hold some of David in it, until they could meet again at the new building. She chose one of the children's toys, a small stuffed dragon which she had worked with before, in a guided visualisation, to symbolise flying away to a safe place. She gladly took it away with her until the next week. David was all the more relieved, as he would not have control over the packing, and such a toy could have been lost in transit. When Amy arrived at the new place, still with boxes in the corridor, she made a home for the dragon on a top shelf, and David made sure it was always there for her session time.

As this example indicates, unforeseen circumstances may require therapists to make special efforts to provide safe and creative therapy. In other circumstances there may be little we can do about the surroundings, but even in a prefab-type room at a surgery we might take in bowls of stones, a pot plant, even a side table lamp to improve the ambience. The point is that the ambience of the framed space is something we need to invest in and build into the creativity of our practice. In private practice we might have the luxury of a dedicated room or a 'neutralised' living area at home – that is, a space free from personal items such as photographs. Clients often remark on the value that the ambience of a setting provides, and may equate us with our setting, and be surprised or disturbed by changes. Of course, when discussing issues about context and setting, we need to be clear about which are our own issues, such as safety and the protection of our personal lives, and which are issues that could be vital for the client, such as respect and value being reflected by the surroundings, and safety and confidentiality being secured.

● ● ● *Pause for thought: your working environment* ● ● ●

- *Are there particular qualities, rooted in your own values, which influence the essential qualities of a space you might work in? In what ways are these qualities limited by circumstances you cannot change?*
- *If you work in an institutional setting, or for an organisation, can you guarantee a regular room booking? Are there things you want to bring in, remove or change around, to provide a therapeutic space, reflecting your values?*
- *If you work at home, what protocols have you established for your space to protect you and keep your attention on the client? What might feel too revealing for you: books, ornaments, photos? Family themselves? Family members being present on the premises?*
- *How do issues of class, money, and other things which clients might deduce or presume from your environmental frame affect your decision about where to work?*

For therapists beginning a practice at home, it is often hard to gauge how to make a contained therapeutic space. It is important that family and home do not impinge too much on our work. What may seem attractive options – to do washing up and phone calls between clients – can end up with us feeling like we never stop being at work. The focus needs to remain ultimately on the client, and we need to keep our personal life intact. We have to develop an instinct, along with our experience, of how this boundary is shaped.

For some people, an institutional setting can feel very constricting in its elaborate and sometimes arcane practices. For others, it provides a container for our creativity, like the artist's studio or the scientific lab. At its best, it can be a place where we can step into our authority and authenticity as a therapist. We need to check in with our core values to see how the setting is aligned with our beliefs. Therapy can be a lonely business, and a shared work setting can be a valuable support for our practice. The following vignette illustrates these concerns.

VIGNETTE: 'ALISON, DAN AND LENA'

Alison, Dan and Lena were all members of a peer supervision group. They each spent part of the week at a complementary therapy centre, but for very different reasons. The rooms were pleasant but multipurpose, needing to be 'set up' each time.

Alison had been looking forward to moving her work to her home for one day a week. A very new client, Nigel, happily moved from the centre and preferred her cosy little living room, with its pictures and flowers. A few sessions in, Nigel noticed that the flowers were a huge bunch of red roses. These, he remarked, were 'obviously a gift to Alison for Valentine's Day', and he speculated about what a kind loving relationship she must have to receive them. In fact, they were an unexpected overture from an ex-boyfriend. Alison felt flushed and agitated, unreasonably intruded upon by Nigel's attention to the flowers, and very foolish for leaving them in the room. Within her humanistic theoretical framework she found a place to enquire about his fantasies about who gives flowers and why.

In supervision, Alison reflected on the incident, both the riskiness of having her complex personal feelings exposed in her home, and the value of the work once she had found her bearings with it. She took the imagery of the flower forward with Nigel, which evolved into some deep work on self love and care, and a few weeks later, Nigel reported that he had bought himself some flowers, and loved 'receiving' them. But in future, Alison checked which personal items might give too much away for her comfort.

Lena had a different issue with work at home. She used the spare bedroom/home office in her flat. It was an easy space to adapt, with a bathroom opposite, and both rooms were near the front door. She needed a practice space at the centre for the days when her partner was in the flat. Her partner's presence would compromise her feeling (if not the fact) of confidentiality, and disturb her concentration. For Lena, it was a question of home life not invading her focus and work-thinking space. The presence of a partner seemed to divide her attention.

Another member, Dan, used the centre for positive reasons of support. He found it good to be in a collegiate relationship with other counsellors and therapists. He liked being able to offload immediate feelings, sharing simple comments with colleagues after a session ('another tough session, after last week's no show!'). This place was also important as somewhere to leave his thoughts and feelings (and notes) *at work*, and not take them back home. He felt he was protecting himself appropriately, and not allowing his real family and children, through their 'things' and 'places' to become part of the client's imaginative world.

What this vignette brings out is how we, as individuals, are the conduit of any environment. Extraordinary sessions have taken place in refugee camps and homeless shelters (Kalmanowitz and Lloyd, 1997: 52). The space that the therapist inhabits in the psyche of the client ideally provides the safety, within and then beyond the session. Safe people make safe places, and we can make a setting safe with our presence. Ultimately it is the people who care for us who will help build our sense of a 'home within'. As the internalised therapeutic boundary extends over time, the client can begin to engage in self-therapy. A person who can feel at home in the world as a whole takes their safety with them. From a transpersonal perspective, if we can reconnect to something greater than ourselves, which we experience as the ground of our being or a 'universal state of consciousness', then it is likely that we will more often feel safe enough (Mindell, 2010: 39). The safe enough space in therapy only becomes possible when the holding frames are secure.

The contractual frame and the therapeutic alliance

Many of the 'housekeeping' contractual issues, such as money, duration of con-tract, and the limits of confidentiality, have been dealt with in Chapter 3. Here we take some space to consider the further creative implications of building a working relationship within the contractual frame. The therapeutic alliance is ostensibly formed in the contract with the adult in front of us. However, this alliance is also established between persons who have developmental histories with all their potential for transference and counter-transference, as we have seen. At times we may need to reaffirm boundaries through a direct and real relationship with each other. At others, we might negotiate shifting the bound-ary when we move into the transpersonal realm, where a more submerged, subtle level can be evoked. Attending to the therapeutic alliance thus requires us to be creatively attentive, within the security of the contractual frame. While the environmental frame contains the *task* of therapy, it is the therapeutic rela-tionship, held by the contract or agreement, which frames the therapeutic *proc-ess*. One of the distinctive aspects of the therapeutic alliance is that it is the adult-to-adult part of the relationship where the terms of therapy can be agreed. This section reflects further on the contractual frame as it supports the development of the therapeutic alliance.

Times, beginnings and endings

Therapeutic modalities have different attitudes to time. Within the range of humanistic traditions, for instance, a therapy session might vary from 50 minutes to one and half hours. As we have seen in Chapter 3, the way a ses-sion begins and ends may also vary considerably. A trainee therapist, for instance, with a 'polite' upbringing, might find it shockingly rude to have their group analytical therapist get up and leave mid-sentence with not a word spoken, or just the comment 'it's time'. Almost in reaction, that trainee therapist might subsequently struggle with making a firm ending with cli-ents. Conversely, the same trainee therapist might learn from this to appreci-ate the value of containment. How the therapist manages the time boundary is often an important indicator, to the client, of that therapist's capacity for safe practice.

It is vital that we are clear about keeping time. Clients will vary hugely in how much time management is needed. Some will feel very anxious about taking too much time, while for others, therapy will move them into a 'right brain' creative modality where clock time is not within their awareness, and they need the therapist to hold time. For the client to drop into the 'serious play' space, the therapist may need to be the 'good enough mother' with count down reminders, like the preparation to end a game before bedtime (Winnicott, 1986: 119). The creativity here is in holding the boundary so we can discover the material that wants to emerge.

● ● ● *Pause for thought: being sensitive to time* ● ● ●

The client's rigid adherence to – or pushing of – a time boundary might be a creative defence against abandonment, invasion, or some issue seeking more direct expression.

- *How might knowledge of such issues affect the way you manage coming in and out of the time frame?*
- *Why do you think clients might adopt different attitudes to the time boundaries you set?*

For some clients, leading chaotic lives, it is an achievement to turn up to therapy at all, and too much of a focus on strict time-keeping might seem punitive to them. In the maternal 'holding' sense, such a client may never have known a safe, bounded play space. We have to 'feed on demand' the infantile part of the client who cannot contain their needs. As time goes on, the value of a routine, and of steady holding, becomes more familiar. There is a gradual enculturation both to the rules of the process of therapy, and the frames within which this process unfolds. Alongside this is the experience of learning that the therapist *is* there, consistently, in ways that are not necessarily evident at first. Equally, some clients do not or cannot afford themselves the space and time for therapy that might be required. In both cases, it may be hard for the client to take in that the therapist has them in mind, when they are not in the room.

Money, time and value

In Chapter 3 we looked at some of the practical, contractual arrangements that various therapists put in place with regard to money and fees. Though money is the most obvious currency of therapy, time is another. Sometimes, especially in private practice, these two currencies are inextricably linked, for example, when sessions are missed. Money and time transactions seem to have many layers of meaning – for therapists and clients.

● ● ● *Pause for thought: time, money and love* ● ● ●

- *Have there been occasions in your life when time or money has become an emblem of love and care?*
- *How might these issues of money, time and love play out in the therapy situation?*

In answer to the first question, you might have considered experiences such as time given to you by a caring friend, when you needed to share some personal concern; or money left to you as a legacy that might have expressed love for you, or alternatively might have been 'earned' by things you had done for the dead person. In all such circumstances, money can have emotional and symbolic meaning. Questions about time and money can stand for how our client feels about scarcity and abundance in general, and can particularly stand in for love: whether it is a finite or a boundless source in the universe to be circulated. Money is also a knotty issue for therapists when setting out in private practice. For instance, it is sometimes difficult for us to charge for therapy, perhaps because therapy is sometimes considered to be an act of altruism or an act of love, and that money somehow takes away from that. However, the other great currency of therapy is self-worth. It seems that the currencies of time, money, and self-worth are inextricably linked, as the following vignette demonstrates.

VIGNETTE: 'ENID AND DARREN'

Enid had been working as a therapist in private practice for some years. With one client she was being challenged about time and money. Darren was a busy probationary year teacher. He often had trouble making time for the session at the end of a mid-week school day, and had cancelled more than once just the day before. He had trouble with priorities at work too, getting to school tired and rushed, then staying on late, taking time with the toughest students.

Enid was both fond of and irritated by this young man. She admired his chutzpah in making it from a rough start in life, and also quietly resented his cavalier use of time and money, happy to spend it on clothes and big nights out to 'unwind'. Was he not bothered enough about therapy? He often complained how little money he got, coming into teaching from sales work. He spent much of the session recounting slights and social minutiae, often bringing up a big question at the end of the session, which he then did not want to follow up next week. Enid found him slippery to get hold of, and he left little room for her.

On this occasion Darren called to say he would be 30 minutes late. Enid reminded him about cancellations, and due notice needed. He was indignant that he had to pay for the whole session when he had explained 'up ahead' that he would only use half the time so she would be able to do something else while she waited. When he arrived he then acknowledged that this was a reflection of his own stress, his need for just such an 'extra' half hour of space in his life. He paid up, got over his indignation, and the theme of feeling undervalued, unseen in some way, came to the fore. At half term, he had rushed back to his parental family home, a long cross-country journey, to see old school friends. He was soon recounting dashing home for weekends, on all sorts of pretexts. Given he was so short of time, Enid pressed him. It emerged that his father, an old-school punishing type, was ill, and, while he said nothing, might not live too long. Darren was angry, not wanting to face the fact that his dad might die with the unresolved resentment remaining between them. Was his father not proud that he had made it into a profession – albeit one he struggled to keep on top of?

●●● *Pause for thought: the currencies of time, money* ●●● *and self-worth*

- *How do you think time and money issues are affecting the therapeutic work in the example above?*
- *How do you see the issue of self-worth as being a theme for both parties in the above vignette? What might be some of the factors contributing to this?*
- *What do you think about the relationship between time, money, and self-worth? You might also think about how you hold these three currencies together in your practice. Perhaps the currency of 'money' is absent in your practice as a volunteer counsellor. You might think if there are any issues around this for you.*

It seems evident that Enid, the therapist, was able to maintain her sense of self-worth by holding boundaries around time and money. The three 'currencies' are interdependent in this example. What is equally evident is that Darren wanted to 'get on' with the work on that occasion when he only had half an hour. Instead, Enid invited Darren to address issues relating to the contractual frame. This also allowed for the transference to be explored between them. Darren could now see the connection between his feeling squeezed by Enid's time boundaries and the restrictions he experienced in his upbringing. He did not feel seen, but felt punished for caring and putting in time with the 'difficult' students. Enid was also aware of the counter-transference: her own feeling that her value was being ignored or discounted paralleled how Darren might also feel at work, and within his family. It is also evident that in returning to a consideration of the contractual frame, Enid was giving Darren a message: 'I am able to hold you'. The fact that Darren could not quite take this in gave Enid an insight. The next layer of transference contains old, unresolved questions for Darren: 'Can't Dad notice me, or give me more time?' This contains an existential issue too: Darren's fear of the possibility of his own early death without leaving his 'mark'.

In that 'half session' Enid could have allowed herself to be more generous, given Darren his free half hour, and for once he would not feel 'hard done by' as he did by his school and family. He might have felt pleased and understood. But if she had not kept the boundary, they might have missed, or taken longer, to get to the deeper existential layers of the work. Enid was perhaps also giving herself a message of 'I am able to hold the frame and the space with us both in it'.

In exploring this vignette, we have highlighted the inter-connectedness of three currencies of therapy: time, money, and self-worth. As therapists, we might consider how we model our appreciation of these currencies to our clients, whether consciously or not. If we bring our own attitudes to money, time and self-worth into awareness, we are arguably more likely to provide a positive model for our clients to internalise.

The embodied relational frame

Therapy is a fully embodied relationship. The tangible presence of another is usually part of the human healing process, and certainly part of the developmental and reparative aspect of therapy. We need to remember that there are two bodies (two animals with all their senses) in the therapy session, and that our own body is a creative instrument of communication and resonance, the living conduit for feelings and imagination. David Abram reminds us of this when he writes: 'Only by entering into relation with others do we effect our own integration and coherence' (2010: 254).

We use discernment in the dynamic process of therapy to listen with all our senses, as well as with our imagination and those internal bodily movements and impulses. Abram writes further that 'it is our bodies that participate in awareness' (2010: 272). Everything is potential information about the therapeutic process. As discussed in Chapter 2, we train ourselves to notice when we are 'opening' as well as when we are 'closing', and consider what this might mean. For instance, we might notice when we maintain an open posture, or notice how and when we are mirroring the client. We might wonder if we are closing off a little, and whether that is to ease the pace or whether we unconsciously disapprove of something.

We might also consider symptoms as containing meaning. For instance, a colleague mentioned working with a client on his right to voice some concerns at work. Half way through the session she began to lose her voice, and felt 'croaky' that evening. This might seem like sympathetic magic going on. But, as Babette Rothschild has pointed out in her book, *Help for the Helper*, it can make sense when thinking about embodied counter-transference, and chronic vicarious trauma (2006: 26, 119).

There is a tendency amongst therapists to be more than usually empathic. However, it is sometimes important to step back a little from the client's process so that we can 'see' what is happening. This is a theme we take up in Chapter 5. We need to find a balance between being subjectively immersed and objectively witnessing. It is more helpful to stand on the bank with a rope than get in the water with a drowning person. There is a notional '50 per cent rule': that it does not serve the client for the therapist to be doing more than half the work in the session. This is also a way of taking care of ourselves, by finding a comfortable emotional distance.

Often, as therapists, we may also need to negotiate keeping the right physical distance. There are other points of contact which might feel 'too close', for instance in the maintaining of appropriate eye contact. We are sometimes taught in training to maintain eye contact, as a means of conveying attentive interest. For many reasons, this level of connection can feel over-invasive to clients, depending on their culture, attachment and relational style. Negotiating these overtures to intimacy can have a profound influence, especially when re-establishing boundaries for a traumatised or abused person, as the next vignette illustrates.

VIGNETTE: 'MAGDA AND SHONA'

One of the issues that Magda brought to Shona was her longing for genuine physical contact, for intimacy rather than repeated brutalising sexual encounters with virtual strangers. Magda had found it hard to be affectionate towards her own children, and she froze when friends offered her a hug. But she longed for cuddles. Shona offered her a large decorative pillow to hold. A shy child emerged from within Magda: she grabbed the pillow, and found herself able to make better eye contact from behind the soft, embracing barrier. She slowly accepted the ordinary needs of her child-within for cuddles. Shona also devised a 'game' for Magda, to enable her to explore real touch in a controlled way. They each drew round their hands on a piece of paper, and then placed the drawings close together. With a paper template which she could move around, Magda felt in control enough to risk putting her hand on the map, next to Shona's hand, then beside it, then, over a few sessions, towards inter-linking fingers. This was the beginning of Magda re-establishing some boundaries which matched her physical body.

When we are working in a reparative and developmental context, it is good to remember that the child can often be activated in the adult and become present in the room. The safe and creative therapist finds a means of embodying meta-phorically a 'holding' care for the child within the adult, while facilitating its development and integration. A client needing such reparative work may often, unwittingly, physically test the boundaries of safety by pushing or manipulating them, replaying past boundary breaches. Our job is to hold the frames which contain the task and process of therapy. This means the contractual frame, expressive of the working alliance, and the embodied relational frame: both contain and support the therapeutic process. As Laurence Spurling (2009: 26) has it, 'what clients seek is containment that is both sanctuary and meaning' and the therapeutic setting aims to provide both.

Negotiation of the physical setting, as in the following vignette, itself restores some more control, establishing therapy as a shared endeavour. This might involve changing the layout of the room. It might also mean keeping coats on, or choosing a room nearer the building exit, or having a view of the window or door. These are all useful physical protective actions. It can be a creative, empowering exercise for the client to be moving chairs or coffee tables to provide channels for communication, barriers for safety or access to escape, as this next vignette suggests.

VIGNETTE: 'TIM AND AMANDA'

When Tim began work with Amanda she soon found it better if they sat at a good distance from each other. He had sought her out as a body psychotherapist, saying he was bringing a history of physical and sexual abuse as a child and six years in the army, where he had seen active service. He could often not notice any fear, but would then unexpectedly recoil in terror. When he first chose a chair next to the door, but quite close to her, she sensed his discomfort. Attending to safety in the room, rather than his body symptoms, she enquired what he liked or disliked about this space. How did he choose where to sit? This opening gave him permission to stop and reflect. He recognised the need to get out easily, so he had chosen a seat that was suitable for a quick escape. He did feel 'too close for comfort' to her though. He found he was more relaxed if she moved her chair away a bit, and didn't feel the need to run. The body work was happening internally. Spending the time on moving chairs around to make the room safe felt playful, and Tim could later experiment with being closer. In due course, they did some hands-on work on his back and belly, helping him establish a slower breathing pattern to calm his frequent panic attacks. It was most important, after these hands-on body episodes, that Amanda return to her chair some distance away, and let Tim settle the new experience into his body boundary undisturbed.

These were very intimate moments, and over time he felt that someone could offer a neutral but loving touch, without their own agenda of exploitation or punishment. It remained crucial in the sessions that he did not have to make any small talk, or friendly hand shakes, or touch Amanda when he handed over his money. This formality kept a safe boundary for him, where he learned all touch would have a therapeutic intent and focus.

It is apparent from this vignette that the therapist is practising within her competency. She is able to discern her client's readiness to explore issues around embodiment. It is worth pausing here to think further about one significant aspect of the fully embodied relational frame.

● ● ● *Pause for thought: physical touch in therapy* ● ● ●

- *In a situation where you are feeling shock or distress, how would you feel if a friend said 'oh come here, let's have hug'? In similar circumstances, how would you feel if your therapist were to offer you physical contact? How would this differ from that of a friend?*
- *Can you think of examples in your own experience where a physical boundary has been crossed for specific reasons? What were the implications at the time, or in subsequent relating?*
- *How do you feel about physical contact arousing sexual feelings in either party, in a therapeutic setting?*

Unlike physical contact between friends, any physical contact between therapists and clients will have a therapeutic import or meaning (Asheri, 2009: 118–19). Handshakes or hugs, as a form of greeting, might seem normal to some clients, but it may be necessary to establish that therapy is a setting in which 'social' touching is not usually appropriate.

It helps to establish your own ground rules for physical contact. A contract about permission to touch is best specifically agreed. Spontaneous touch without discussion in therapy holds a danger of becoming like other kinds of intimacy, including the sexual. There may be a frisson of 'no going back'. Thus it is important to be clear about the purpose of the physical contact, and to have time to reflect and feed back about the ongoing effect. Sexual feelings may occur, but denial or disapproval can retrigger a client's early shame about their childlike aliveness, as discussed earlier in this book. As therapists, we have a power that is often experienced by clients as parental, and therefore our task is to accept the erotic charge but not act upon it (Eiden, 2002: 38–9).

Extending therapeutic frames

In an ideal world, we would always wish to discuss the extending of one or more of these frames with a colleague or supervisor before taking action that might threaten a client's security, or our own. But staying in our literal safety zone is not always possible or even desirable when, like any creative activity, therapy sometimes crosses conventions – for what seem like reasons of therapeutic necessity. As well as this, accidents happen to human beings. We get a double-booked room, lose our keys, have our own emergencies, forget an appointment, or mis-attune. The issue then is a matter of how we might mend a frame that has been temporarily broken. This is a matter that is taken up in Chapter 5, when discussing more serious instances of therapeutic breakdown. There are times, however, when we need to trust our creativity and resourcefulness, as we see in the next vignette.

VIGNETTE: 'LEILA AND ISABEL'

Leila was expecting her usual day at her practice in winter, when she discovered the heating had broken down. Staying in the room was not an option; it was freezing, and the arrival of the heating engineer would disturb any work. It was too late to cancel her first client, Isabel. Should she turn her away on arrival, and leave her client disappointed, with a wasted journey? Or could they retrieve the time? Leila remembered Isabel talking about her missed opportunities for fun, not stopping to play with the grandchildren, nor spending time on walks by the river with her husband. A theme of disappointment ran through Isabel's therapy.

Soon, Isabel arrived well wrapped against the cold. A good thing too, as it offered a way out. 'We could go to the café', Leila said, 'but it will be crowded and not at all confidential. How about that walk by the river you talked about?' Isabel jumped at the suggestion, and added that they could collect bread from the café and go and feed the ducks. The energy was transformed, and the next hour was spent with Isabel teaching her therapist about ducks and their habits, playful and contactful, reminding her of just how she wanted to be with her grandchildren and husband.

It was a risk – they were moving outside of the safety of the room. Leila might have been dodging the reality of letting her client down, and the inadequacy of her holding therapeutic space. If she had cancelled, they could, next week, have worked with the disappointment and any transferential issues involved, such as Leila embodying Isabel's mother with her strictures and fearfulness and reasons not to do things. By going out, however, they broke through to a new creative place, to re-engage in a love of life which Isabel had felt she was on the verge of losing.

As in this vignette, there are times when 'stuff happens' and one of the frames is challenged, in this instance the environmental frame. If someone arrives dripping wet after being caught in a cloudburst, should the therapist offer a towel to dry hair, and a place for wet shoes? If a disabled client needs to be fetched from therapy, should a therapist enforce the boundary while the client waits like an infant or a parcel? Would it not be more dignified to assist them down the path to a waiting car, even if this does mean engaging with a husband or friend? Dilemmas like these, and the one which follows, might be usefully explored in supervision.

Pause for thought: how many in the room?

A client has a new baby four weeks early, which means she misses the ending session before a planned break. She then wants to come anyway to tidy up loose ends, to talk about the unexpected drama, and also wants to show off the baby. How would you respond, and why?

There are many points to consider here. Would you expect the client to come along with or without the child to make such an ending? Perhaps you would think of mother and baby as still in a sense 'one', not yet wholly separate (Winnicott, 1986: 72). In that case, you would need to be prepared for a 'family' therapy session, rather than an individual one. Given the transferential dimension, you might also want to consider how your client may compare your manner with her baby, with that of its real grandparents. There are many possibilities for relational growth here, but we would also need an awareness of such issues. If, on the other hand, you objected to her bringing the baby, might this be rejecting her real infant as not good enough compared to her 'internal infant' present in therapy? The baby would take attention from the mother – delightful perhaps, but not leaving much space for mum alone. Would you postpone the session, until she felt happy to come alone, which might risk leaving her with unfinished business? If so, how might you negotiate this?

Attention to our core values in supervision, taking time to step back and reflect on our practice as a whole, will keep us exercising the creative muscle required to make spontaneous decisions. We can then choose to negotiate extending the frame, or to re-frame the meaning of an experience, or to re-frame the mode of relationship, in the service of deeper values. Such shifts of frame are often required when we move from one relational mode to another. This is perhaps especially true when we move into the transpersonal realm, as we can see in the following vignette.

VIGNETTE: 'HERMIONE AND CAROLINE'

Hermione was a mature client, who had chosen to commit to a further two years of therapy after the required hours of therapy training. She and her therapist Caroline were aware of similarities in their lifestyle. Now they were both therapists, of course, but they also both loved playing the piano and gardening, and metaphors from both music and nature had enriched the work. Caroline was concerned not to share too much about herself, and yet, there was a natural resonance between them, in their imagery and language.

Each year, Hermione brought a sprig of her favourite winter-flowering Daphne shrub that grew by her back door. The established ritual was to receive the gift, which was the scent, and for Hermione to have someone else understand how it lifted her spirits. It reminded her of the warm jasmine scent of childhood on another continent. They treated it as a found object, rather than a present. However, Caroline kept the cuttings and some had rooted.

One winter, Hermione's shrub suffered in the cold and damp, and its refusal to flower echoed her despair. Hopes of a reunion with her diaspora family before the expected death of her aunt were fading. Plans for a new job were dashed. Caroline invited Hermione through visualisation to go into the dark place of the earth, to connect with the place into which things die away, and explore what might be reborn. Then Caroline remembered seeing the first buds on her almond tree opening up that lunchtime, in her garden. She spoke of how the tree had been trapped in a pot during rebuilding, and failed to flower the previous year. Now it had new ground, and was returning to health. This personal disclosure was also about transpersonal themes. In the dark, they went out to find the tree, to feel as much as see the very first small flowers. Hermione said it felt like a message shared from the Earth itself: 'you and your family have been uprooted, but you might find new place, and blossom one day soon'.

When Hermione completed her therapy the following autumn, it was Caroline who brought a gift to her. One of the Daphne cuttings was returned. Caroline explained that it symbolized for her how one invests in therapy, and then the investment is returned from the 'safekeeping' of the therapist. At this moment a 'threshold' opened onto existential and transpersonal meaning (Hyde, 2007: 23, 44–7). A couple of gardeners, exchanging their mutual delight in nature, found a way towards a deeper understanding of their relationship, nurtured by a universal being held by Nature, a force larger than both of them.

This vignette demonstrates that with discernment and awareness the therapist is able to extend the frames of therapy. Extending a frame is different from breaking it, and there is always a risk that the frames might break. One important difference is that extending a frame allows more of life and its potential to enter in, whereas breaking a frame threatens both these things. Was it wrong for Caroline to take Hermione out to the garden, down slippery steps in the dark? All sorts of risk assessments would have said it was, but the symbolism of taking a risk was part of the action. Equally, so was the returning of the gift that had been held in trust – the cutting, now rooted enough to survive alone.

Chapter summary

We have been exploring different frames for the task and process of therapy. These frames overlap and are interconnected. The environmental frame provides a safe and creative space for therapy, physically, emotionally and interpersonally. The contractual frame supports the development of a therapeutic alliance, which in turn provides a basis for the development of a deep, embodied relationship between client and therapist. The creative process of therapy is bounded by the safety which these frames provide. We have also highlighted three interrelated currencies – time, money, and self worth – which must be honoured to protect the integrity of the therapeutic process.

Further reading

Gray, A. (1994) *An Introduction to the Therapeutic Frame*. London and New York: Routledge. Gray makes an analogy between the 'therapeutic frame' and the 'mother-infant container', seeing the frame first and foremost as a safe container for the client's – and the therapist's – anxiety.

Hartley, L. (ed.) (2009) *Contemporary Body Psychotherapy: The Chiron Approach*. London: Routledge. A primer and overview of relational work, which addresses issues wider than body psychotherapy alone.

Orbach, S. (2000) *The Impossibility of Sex*. London: Penguin. This book offers very readable essays on boundaries and relationship, written from a psychoanalytic viewpoint.

Shaw, R. (2003) *The Embodied Psychotherapist: The Therapist's Body Story*. Hove and New York: Brunner-Routledge. Based on a research survey of therapists across theoretical modalities, this investigates bodily counter-transference experience in therapist self-care, and in creative work with clients.

CHAPTER 5

DEALING WITH MISTAKES IN THERAPEUTIC PRACTICE

The inevitability of making mistakes

The complex nature of human relationships means that within them mistakes can happen and difficulties can sometimes arise. The therapeutic relationship is not exempt from the inevitability of mistakes, and their consequences. It is perhaps a paradox of therapy that the therapeutic relationship can ignite the same hurts which the person came into therapy to resolve. This may be especially true when the therapist takes their eye away from the subtle dynamics of the transferential dimension. Fortunately, mistakes can also be opportunities for healing and further growth if the relationship survives the initial rupture or conflict, and can then be worked through to a new place.

It seems that some therapists do not anticipate mistakes or ruptures occurring in their practice. We therefore do not always know how to seek supportive processes, other than supervision, when the therapy loses integrity or boundedness, or when the relationship begins to break down. Sometimes this is so because of the therapist's fear – conscious or unconscious – of considering the possibility of mistakes. At other times it might be due to a lack of confidence, or naiveté, or over-confidence. Or sometimes we are just not sure where to turn if we have concerns about possible ethical problems in our practice.

This chapter begins from the assumption that mistakes in therapy are inevitable, and it discusses some of the aspects of the therapeutic framework which may be vulnerable to mistakes or mis-attunement. Mis-attunement here refers to that commonly experienced process of empathically missing or not 'seeing' the felt and usually unspoken narrative of the client (Gilhooley, 2011: 311–33). It can arise out of the therapist's mistaken assumptions, observations and interpretations, as we will see. As well as considering ways to minimise mistakes, we are going to explore some of the available professional supports which offer ethical and creative ways of encouraging movement through mistakes, rather than getting stuck in their aftermath. We give some examples to illustrate how formal complaints may arise, and conclude with a reflective vignette which follows a mediation process from initial complaint through to resolution.

It is worth re-emphasising that our motivation here does not arise out of a wish to encourage therapists to be defensive or self-protective, but out of a belief that safe and creative practice requires us to be familiar with the structures, procedures, and processes designed to support both participants in the therapy. As we have made clear in earlier chapters of this book, rather than taking a quasi-legalistic view of ethics, we are arguing for the development of a therapist's practical wisdom. This view prioritises the development of therapeutic ethics from the ground up, rather than the application of pre-established rules. We argue that safe and creative practice requires our capacity for remaining non-defensively open to exploration despite the vulnerability that this might bring.

Factors which cause mistakes to gradually emerge or suddenly erupt in therapy are usually to do with boundary disturbance or violation, or are the result of what we might call methodological mistakes or mis-attunement. However, therapist intentionality is also a factor to be taken into account when thinking about 'mistakes'. As therapists we may not be wholly aware of our motivations or intentions, and this is where supervision and personal therapy play a significant role in raising our awareness. In discussing these issues, we will first consider boundary disturbance or violation, and methodological mistakes or mis-attunement. Then, in our next section we will look at other features of the therapeutic relationship which are sometimes susceptible to mistakes or ruptures.

Boundary disturbance or violation

Mistakes in therapy most frequently occur within the cornerstone area of boundaries, and boundary values. The following vignette looks at a situation where the boundary provided by the valuing of 'client autonomy' is breached.

VIGNETTE: 'JOHN AND STEPHEN'

John, a man in his early twenties, came to therapy burdened by the emotional weight of his two overpowering parents. They were both intellectually quite intense, and would frequently argue about minor things: who said what to each other, how it was said, and when. This had been going on for many years, and because of it John felt it difficult to get close to either of his parents, and often found it unbearable to be in the family home. He was reasonably close to his two siblings, a younger brother and sister, both of whom, like John, were academically bright. The atmosphere at home was often 'heavy', and father, now retired, was at home more often. There were often long spells when either parent would not speak to the other.

During a particularly difficult session, John was expressing concerns that his parents' intensity felt tantamount to emotional abuse, and that his father had particularly abused him in this way. John had packed his bags, in anticipation of leaving home, while his parents were on holiday. Stephen, his therapist, decided to take a risk. Given that John had said that he might not be able to confront his parents, Stephen took it upon himself, without permission, to write to John's parents informing them: 'It is unfortunate, but John has chosen not to have further contact with you for at least two years. He will not be telling you where he is going, and does not want you to try and make contact. The reason for this is because he has been emotionally abused by both of you since he was five.' Stephen posted this letter to John's parents one day after the session. John did leave home, and 10 years later has not seen or spoken to either of them. They often discuss the possibility of raising a complaint against Stephen, who now lives in another country.

The violation of client autonomy is alarmingly evident in this vignette. You can probably see where Stephen was acting out a 'good parent' counter-transference to protect John from further abuse. At the same time, though, he was manipulating John into making a decision, and making sure this was carried out, by intervening himself. Stephen was in this way also being abusive. Despite knowing full well the limitations of the therapist's role, there are times when we might feel unwilling to be a silent bystander, colluding in the face of obvious abuse. We may be tempted to 'rescue' the client from a situation that causes them to feel anger, disempowerment, disappointment, or desperation. Let us think about this further.

● ● ● *Pause for thought: consequences of rescuing* ● ● ●

- *What thoughts and feelings do you have about this vignette?*
- *What might be the hidden motives of Stephen's action?*
- *What are your views about the ethics of acting out of counter-transference issues?*

Reading this account may have made you aware of your own 'rescuing' tendencies. Perhaps you felt angry on John's behalf, or remembered family experiences of your own. We all develop 'touch points' which can lead to us having our own agenda on such matters. Sometimes the therapist's own issues obstruct the course of therapy and it becomes difficult to be alongside rather than leading, or we are drawn into rescuing, rather than enabling our client. Often the role of the therapist as compassionate witness gets forgotten. If John had been allowed to experience his full range of feelings in relation to this dilemma in the presence of an attentive therapist, he might have found his own way forward when he was ready. The downside of empathy, if there is one, is that the same feelings that John struggles with can arise sympathetically in the therapist, who quite understandably does not want to feel them. We need to learn to contain these intense feelings rather than act them out through rescuing. Rescuing is often, after all, not much more than a way of rescuing oneself from an unbearable experience. So John left home without resolving his core issue of finding a way of confronting his parents, in particular his father. It was done *for* him; or you might say, done *to* him, for he was left without an authentic resolution. It is possible to imagine the positive strength which may have grown in John if, for instance, Stephen had been able to support him in standing up to his parents without deliberately hurting them in any way.

What about the ethics of the therapist acting out of the counter-transference? Perhaps Stephen, a bit like John's real father, was unable to find that delicate balance of meeting his client at a relational depth, while at the same time allowing him full autonomy in decision making. Perhaps this was, in part, a genuine mistake on Stephen's part, though it is likely that he would have been aware of deliberately over-stepping boundaries. Perhaps, too, Stephen was only wanting the best for John, though it is likely that there was self-interest in there too.

Other ethical issues might arise when a therapist acts out of a counter-transference experience. Such disturbances might include extending sessions without negotiation, breaking confidentiality without good reason, terminating therapy without prior discussion or notification, or talking about the therapist's own issues in the session. Of course, boundary disruptions might be more subtle, and include, for instance, a question felt as intrusive, or a persistent interpretation which the client resents or refuses to accept. You will be able to think of other violations or disruptions.

Boundary violations not only relate to emotional and psychological manipulation or abuse, they also include a range of behaviours which undermine the autonomy and well-being of the client (and sometimes the therapist). Some examples in previous chapters have shown how problems can arise over money and fees. Another obvious and highly damaging form of boundary violation is sexual exploitation. In such cases, the therapist may be acting out feelings of loneliness, lust, or a need to rescue, or might be susceptible to flattery or to their client's seductive qualities, or may have gone beyond a considered intervention of touch. It is sobering to note that one study (Russell, 1993) found that therapists' sexual exploitation of clients occurred most often in circumstances where the client was trying to work through previous sexually abusive experiences. Such unresolved traumatic experiences in the client can intensify counter-transference responses in the therapist, who may end up re-enacting, in a sense, the original abuse. As Lynne Gabriel (2005: 22–34) notes, these re-abusing experiences seem particularly damaging to clients, even if they do eventually find the resources to complain against a sexually exploitative therapist.

It is important to remember, however, that erotic energy also contains a desire for growth. We might remind ourselves that the term 'erotic' comes from Eros, who is not only the Greek god of romantic love but also the god of life energy and potential. If Eros is understood as the bringer of creative energy, the necessary energy for change, of purpose, of going somewhere, it is inevitable that 'Eros' energy will be present in therapy at some point or other. This interpretation acknowledges the transpersonal dimension of love in therapy.

Dialogue between a client and therapist about their personal experience of the 'erotic' is not necessarily to be avoided, as we saw in Chapter 3. But the ethical question remains as to what the therapist does with feelings and stirrings in such circumstances. Boundaries are obviously crucially important here. The point to stress is that it is always the therapist's responsibility to deal with a situation in which their own sexual feelings may be activated by a client. Because therapy is a unique relationship, sexual boundaries and erotic feelings have different meanings than in ordinary life situations. The people concerned are not 'just two adults': they are adults in a relationship where everything is given meaning related to the therapeutic process. In order to work ethically and creatively with 'Eros' and the erotic, we need to continue to explore this territory for ourselves, in personal therapy and supervision, through reading and further training, as well as exploring these issues with clients. You might find the 'further reading' section at the end of this chapter helpful as a start.

Methodological mistakes

Another kind of mistake arises out of methodology, or the 'doing' of therapy. In using the term 'methodological mistake', we mean a mistake or rupture which does not necessarily transgress a boundary but nevertheless causes a rupture in the therapeutic process. These are often mis-attunements, as demonstrated in the following brief vignette.

VIGNETTE: 'REBECCA AND STEPHANIE'

When Rebecca reported that her abuser at the age of six had been her mother, her therapist, Stephanie, was taken by surprise, and momentarily looked away. 'You don't believe me', Rebecca remarked. 'What makes you think that?' Stephanie replied. 'Because I could see the disbelief in your eyes', Rebecca retorted. Stephanie responded straightaway by explaining that she *did* believe Rebecca's disclosure, and that she was puzzled why Rebecca thought otherwise. At this point Rebecca picked up her bag and said tearfully 'I think I would like to stop the session now'.

Stephanie's 'doing' mistake was that her intervention – what she said in response to Rebecca – was not empathic. While no boundary was broken or violated, for Rebecca it felt quite the opposite. Rebecca's vulnerability, at the moment of disclosure, meant that not being seen or heard had the feeling of something broken in the therapeutic process. This obviously had a negative impact on her sense of relationship with her therapist. There are a number of alternative ways in which Stephanie might have responded, such as mirroring what Rebecca might have felt, acknowledging the felt shock at hearing this rather than leaving the 'surprise' to be interpreted as 'disbelief'. Stephanie might have resisted her defensive need to 'explain', and allowed herself to get in touch with her own vulnerability, and then found a way of communicating from this experience. At some much later point, Stephanie might have enquired whether not being believed was a familiar experience for Rebecca. Perhaps the most important way of minimising this empathic mistake might have been through offering an 'opening' rather than 'closing' intervention. For example, Stephanie might have responded to Rebecca, saying 'Oh, I'm a bit surprised you say that. Can you say a little more about what that was like, when you saw disbelief in my eyes?' This might have helped Rebecca to feel Stephanie was still interested in how she, Rebecca, was feeling.

This is a good place to turn our attention to the wider relational field within which mistakes and ruptures occur.

Minimising mistakes in the therapeutic field

Mistakes which disrupt the therapeutic process often arise out of partially unconscious processes. Such processes include, in particular, negative transference, projective identification, and resistance. These matters are discussed in some detail in Rowan and Jacobs (2002). Such concepts have their origins, of course, in the psychoanalytic approach to therapy. Basically, psychoanalytic or psychodynamic therapists will view these processes as well recognised phenomena, events and stages over the course of a long therapy. The transference relationship is expected to go through many challenges and changes of this kind, as the client comes to a greater understanding of themselves as a human being in relationship. These processes are described in detail by psychoanalysts such as Jeffrey Seinfeld (1990) or Phil Mollon (2002) who have given critical accounts of their client work.

The understanding of processes like negative transference, projective identification and resistance is not as clear cut as this across the range of therapeutic approaches. For example, humanistic and integrative therapists are more likely to use these terms to denote a client's attempts to relate to their therapist at times when they are unable to communicate directly about intense or otherwise difficult feelings and experiences. The task for the humanistic or integrative therapist is not just to support the client in recognising what they might be doing when they relate in such a way. It is also to try and address these issues together, as relational processes to which therapist and client are both contributing. The aim is to bring the client and therapist back to the 'real relationship' of two equal adults, not, as in psychoanalysis, to go with the life cycle of the transference until it is resolved.

Wherever our own particular therapeutic approach fits within the range of different therapeutic modalities, it is likely that these processes present some of the greatest challenges for the beginner therapist as well as the more experienced practitioner.

Negative transference

No therapist likes to be caught up in the field of negative transference. Generally speaking, this field is charged by the client's experience of the therapist as, for instance, a controlling, devaluing, or punitive parent. This can be difficult to sit with and work through, and the therapist may be personally susceptible to the client's expressions of suspicion, distrust, or annoyance. The activation of negative transference requires the therapist's capacity to stay with the process rather than to fearfully disengage from it through defensiveness or a desire for approval. As we have seen, defensive practice is fear-based practice. Staying *with* the process presumes the therapist's ability, first to notice what is happening in the relational field, and then to experience this in the present moment. That is, be opening rather than closing. It can be a mistake to adopt a defensive position, as our last vignette illustrated. The next vignette offers an example of staying with and working through a difficult process.

VIGNETTE: 'CAROLINE AND ROBERT'

Caroline attended weekly sessions with Robert for three years as part of her training as a therapist. An important theme which ran throughout the therapy was her experience of abandonment by her father when she was 12. While she was outwardly accepting of this, she inwardly felt angry towards him, and often felt insecure in her relationships with men. During a particularly difficult conversation about self-worth, after Robert had returned from a two-week holiday, Caroline questioned Robert's commitment to her process.

Caroline: I think … [*silence*] … that you would like it if I discontinued my therapy.

Robert: [*silence*] It's really difficult for you right now. I can feel it's a struggle.

Caroline: I don't think this process is working for me [*prepares to leave the session*].

Robert: I think it might be really useful if we were to try to find out what's going on, Caroline, but of course you are also free to leave.

Caroline: I really don't think you want me here [*standing up*].

Robert: Caroline, this is difficult for me too. I would really like to try to understand what's going on between us. [*Caroline sits on the edge of her seat looking away.*] It might help to try to understand what's going on.

Caroline: Yes.

Robert: [*silence*] It sounds as if when we talk about your struggles with valuing yourself that you experience me as being like your father who didn't care. Perhaps you also thought that my going on holiday meant that I didn't care [*Caroline begins to cry*]. And feeling this seems painful for you.

The conversation continued, considering how her father's abandonment left Caroline with a tendency to activate feelings of rejection, and how this might be brought into the therapeutic relationship.

One of the important themes in this vignette is Robert's capacity to remain open, receptive and non-defensive. Moreover, he allows the process to unfold naturally, without trying to influence what is happening. But he feels it his responsibility to contain the process, as far as he is able, by referring to the collaborative nature of therapy through the use of the pronoun 'we'. He also talks about commitment through his 'therapeutic use of self', or his capacity to use an aspect of himself as a therapeutic intervention (Wosket, 1999: 11). Robert's disclosure of something being 'difficult for me too' is an example of this. The fundamental point here is that the use of self is in the service of the therapy, and not about the therapist.

Pause for thought: negative transference

Either on your own, with a colleague, or in a group, think about or discuss the following questions.

- *Can you identify examples from your own practice which might indicate the activation of negative transference – or negative counter-transference? How, if at all, was this brought out in the therapy?*
- *What might be some of the challenges of sitting with and working through negative transference?*

In answer to the first question, you might have recalled a time when you perhaps felt somewhat mean towards a client who themselves seemed parsimonious or greedy with time or money. Or maybe you remembered feeling bored or tired when with a client who was especially narcissistic or, alternatively, trying to keep themselves hidden from you. The often embodied experience of transference means that it is useful for the therapist to take account of a range of bodily-felt experiences, as possible indications of issues that might be relevant for the therapy. One of the challenges therapists often encounter in working with negative transference or counter-transference is the fear that acknowledging it might damage a 'good' therapeutic relationship. You might have doubted or been unsure about the therapeutic benefit of exploring negative transference, or felt that it was not appropriate to do so in brief counselling. But consider what positive outcomes might result, for instance, from a therapist finding a way to name and challenge a friendless client's 'mean-ness' or 'boring-ness'. If done in a way that meant the therapist could own their own part in the process, such a client might well see that they had some responsibility themselves for being friendless. These are issues worth exploring in your peer group or in supervision. If we ignore negative transference, we invite further problems into the relationship. If we work with it, on the other hand, creative and collaborative resolutions become possible.

Projective identification

Another process which can become activated in therapy is projective identification. This occurs when a client who is unable to acknowledge their own difficult feelings, unconsciously projects them into the therapist, who then becomes the 'accepting' therapist and experiences feelings or sensations which they do not recognise as belonging to themselves (Waska, 2008: 336). The therapist comes to recognise this interpersonal phenomenon through careful scrutiny of their own subjective experience in the moment, and through clarifying this with the client, to get to the root of whose feelings are being made aware in this way. However, there is also a possibility that the therapist might identify too strongly with the feelings, as if they *do* belong to him or her.

VIGNETTE: 'WENDY AND SIMONE'

While listening to Wendy talking about the details of her younger brother's protracted illness and sudden death five years earlier, her therapist, Simone, began to feel profoundly sad. Finding it increasing difficult to contain her feelings Simone wondered what might be going on. At first she thought that these feelings were about her own losses. But having explored this fully in her own therapy, she suspected that it must mostly be about something else. Wondering whether Wendy was unconsciously defending herself against painful feelings of unresolved grief which she also wanted the therapist to know about, Simone asked Wendy how she was feeling about the loss of her brother. At this point Wendy burst into tears, and Simone's sadness left.

It is probable that Wendy's 'talking' was a defence against experiencing some unbearable 'feelings', which were being projected into Simone. It would have been a mistake for Simone to have dismissed her feelings of sadness as not belonging to the therapeutic process. But it would also have been a mistake not to have wondered whether the sadness was about herself. With any form of defence, resistance is often part of it.

Resistance

It is useful to remind ourselves that the purpose of a defence is self-protection. We might argue further that defences are our innate creative capacity to cope with seemingly unbearable or impossible circumstances, and are to be respected. The activation of a defence often signifies that something important is being kept out of awareness, or hidden from consciousness, because of associated feelings of fear, anxiety, or shame. Getting too close to that 'something' often activates resistance, and it is likely that resistance is one defensive process which often masks other deeper defences. The following 'pause for thought' invites you to consider this.

● ● ● *Pause for thought: resistance* ● ● ●

- *Think about ways in which resistance is present in therapy.*
- *Consider ways in which you might sit with or work through resistance, while also respecting its purpose.*

It is important to remind ourselves that both participants in the therapy are susceptible to resistance. We often recognise resistance as a feeling of being 'defensive', but as we have seen with Wendy, it can also manifest itself in other ways. As might be familiar from our personal therapy experience, resistance is something to work with and through. Working with resistance requires tentatively naming the process which the resistance is bringing to your attention in that moment, and negotiating ways of collaboratively working through this, as the following vignette demonstrates.

VIGNETTE: 'FRANK AND MATHEW'

Recently Frank had been either late for therapy, or had telephoned to postpone or re-arrange sessions, or had cancelled at the last minute. Being aware of Frank's possible ambivalence about therapy, his therapist, Mathew, tentatively enquired whether Frank was also wondering whether their late start that evening was serving an important purpose which they were both unable to see at that moment. After allowing Frank to consider this for a few moments, Mathew continued the discussion as follows:

Mathew: I am wondering whether you might like to consider this further.

Frank: [silent for a while – his hesitation maybe indicating that he was now experiencing his resistance]

Mathew: This is difficult for you …

Frank: Yes …

Mathew: Is it alright to continue?

Frank: Yes …

Mathew: You might want to check that out with what you are *feeling*.

Frank: The feeling says 'no, don't go there'.

Mathew: OK. [*long silence*]

Frank: This is difficult … [*looking at Mathew*]

Mathew: I can *feel* that … [*pause*]. I am wondering whether there's an image for what you are finding difficult …

Frank: A 'gate'. I see an image of a 'gate'.

[*After exploring this image for a while …*]

Frank: I guess the way the gate opens as I approach it means that I am ready to finish therapy, but know this will be difficult for me because it … [*begins to cry*] … means that I need to face losing you … [*crying more fully*] … just as I lost my father … [*crying even more fully*] …

Mathew also feels the welling up of tears, and both sit acknowledging the sadness about the prospect of ending their relationship. Later on, they agree that they will need to set aside time, over the coming sessions, to negotiate how best to do this.

While this is not the only way of working with and through resistance, this style of intervention was useful for Frank. You will notice that Mathew invites Frank to get a sense of whether the 'yes' was coming from his 'feeling' rather than his 'thinking', given that Frank was experiencing his resistance rather than wondering about it. Mathew interpreted Frank's 'look' as a willingness to persevere, but requiring some assistance. Trusting his intuition regarding the implications of a direct confrontation, Mathew decided to work with image rather than directly with feeling. This was a creative risk, as he did not know how useful this intervention might be at that moment. Abraham Maslow is reported to have said that if we only have a hammer we treat everything as if it is a nail. The important intention underpinning creative therapy is not to be clever or formulaic, but to make use of the imagination to enable the emergence of something which is ready to come into view. To this extent psychotherapy is a form of midwifery.

Aiming to minimise mistakes can lead to defensive practice. Therefore, balancing this with creative risk-taking, as Mathew does here, is important. The point to stress is that we need to be able to deal non-defensively with mistakes when they occur. As writers like Patrick Casement (2002) suggest, most mistakes which disrupt the process of therapy can be worked through whilst remaining therapeutically in relationship. On other occasions, mistakes can only be resolved by enlisting different kinds of support, as we will now consider.

Ethical review as a support for safe and creative practice

Ethical reviews are a relatively new kind of support for therapists. The UK Association for Humanistic Psychology Practitioners (UKAHPP) offers a pioneering example of this (www.ahpp.org/ethical/review_procedure.htm), and their model has inspired other organisations to consider offering practitioners a similar opportunity.

Briefly, an ethical review is a conversation with an 'outsider', usually also a member of an Ethics Committee, to review a problematic issue. The aim is to enable practitioners to review their practice in relation to a whole range of issues which cannot be fully considered, contained or resolved within supervision. Examples might include seeking support with integrating a new training into existing practice, such as ecopsychology with psychotherapy, or considering ethical dilemmas which may have arisen for the therapist. It is a place where the parties meet as equals, or where the therapist can 'forward think', to imagine what ethical issues might be unearthed by a proposed boundary shift or other change. The following vignette offers an example of a concern which might be considered in an ethical review.

VIGNETTE: 'KAREN AND JENNIFER'

Karen, a trainee counsellor, entered into therapy as part of her training requirement, but also because of a desire to explore how she might realise more of her potential in life, especially in relation to her creativity. Knowing that her therapist, Jennifer, was interested in working with dreams and the imagination through image making, she quickly began to immerse herself in the therapeutic process. A key theme in therapy was Karen's early life experience of a punishing mother, who often dismissed Karen's creativity as 'a flight into fancy'. After three years of working together, Karen wondered if she might end therapy but then enter into a supervisory relationship with Jennifer, as the creative perspectives of Jennifer's practice were of interest to her. After negotiating a three-month transitional gap, a date for the first supervision session was arranged. Five months into monthly supervision Jennifer found it necessary to question Karen's boundaries in relation to a young woman she was counselling, suggesting that Karen was acting out the counter-transference of a 'good mother' by being overly flexible around boundaries. Taken aback by this apparent challenge, Karen was suddenly reminded of her punishing mother, and felt overwhelmed by this.

Both practitioners wondered whether it was a mistake to have made the transition from a therapeutic to a supervisory relationship, and Jennifer agreed to bring this to ethical review.

Pause for thought: ethical review

Think about the following questions arising from the vignette you have just read.
* How might the mistake have been avoided?
* What do you think about the ethics of this relationship transition?

It might be argued that the relationship transition should never have been considered on the grounds that a transference relationship in therapy is never fully resolved. Here, for instance, it might lead Karen to be deferential to Jennifer's opinion, or to attach the notion of punishment to Jennifer's critical interventions. The meaning that the therapist holds for the client, and the felt memory of the healing relationship, continues to be effective even after the therapy has ended. It might be argued that this potential benefit is undone if the two parties engage in a non-therapeutic relationship, such as supervision, which by virtue of how the relationship began, can never be equal. However, it might also be argued that if Jennifer and Karen were to agree to continue to be open with each other in their new relationship, and if Karen were able to re-enter therapy with a separate therapist, then it might be possible for the supervisory relationship with Jennifer to continue. The acknowledgment of a possible mistake meant that there was an amicable way forward with this. Both practitioners were unable to know what might unfold within the new supervisory relationship, and there was important learning to be gained from activating an ethical review.

How complaints can arise

Many complaints arise when the kinds of mistakes or mis-attunements we have been discussing are not openly and fully addressed in the therapeutic relationship, with a view towards understanding and resolving the difficulty. The following vignette is an example of this.

VIGNETTE: 'VIVIENNE AND PETER'

Vivienne entered into therapy with Peter one year ago, wishing to find a way forward with her long-standing sense of dissatisfaction with life. Despite running her own busy counselling practice and having been in extensive therapy during her training, Vivienne still felt that there was more that needed to be addressed in therapy. Over several sessions, Peter wondered whether Vivienne was depressed, and suggested that this might be because she had not fully grieved the loss of her father, who had died a few years ago. When Vivienne replied that she did not think this was the issue, Peter suggested that she could be resisting this fact. Thinking that Peter must be right, she decided to visit her GP, but in doing so she realised that feelings of anger were rising up in her. When discussing this with Peter, he thought that this anger might in fact be due to Vivienne's unresolved grief. Vivienne was not so sure herself about this but went along with Peter's suggestions.

A few months later, Vivienne read an article on positive transference, and realised what was happening: Peter had 'become' her lost father who she wanted to please, and whose expectations she was unable to meet. She wondered too whether Peter was acting out her 'father' in the counter-transference. Moreover, it gradually dawned on Vivienne that her dissatisfaction with life was itself partly due to unfinished 'father' issues that her therapy with Peter had so far failed to address.

When she eventually confronted Peter with her new understanding he was unable to accept her viewpoint because he was fixed in his belief that his position was theoretically correct. Moreover, he was convinced that Vivienne's resistance further supported his position. Still prepared to believe Peter's perspective, Vivienne became increasingly 'stuck' in the therapy, before deciding to finish. A few months later Vivienne was urged by a colleague to raise a complaint against Peter.

What is apparent in this vignette is that despite Vivienne rejecting Peter's interpretation, Peter persisted in his own belief that he was right. This prompted him to interpret Vivienne's rejection as resistance, rather than take this an opportunity for further collaborative exploration. He clung to his interpretation of Vivienne, rather than addressing the reality of her experience. It is also apparent that Vivienne had arrived at an important insight into her life dilemma, and that her feelings of anger might have been evidence of this. It also appears that Peter mismanaged the transference, thereby perpetuating the 'powerful father/compliant daughter' dynamic. Let us consider this vignette in a bit more detail.

●●● *Pause for thought: avoiding complaints* ●●●

- *How do you think Peter's mis-attunement might have been minimised, and what might help him to avoid similar mistakes in the future?*

Perhaps you thought that Peter should have been more open to collaborative enquiry rather than being defensively fixed on his own perspective. Or, he might have been unconsciously protecting himself against the negative transference of Vivienne's feelings towards her father. Peter might benefit from further supervision and training in working with and through transference. It is always useful to ask for other therapists to help you 'spot' when you are being caught up in transferential issues, because, in their very nature, they are often out of our ordinary awareness.

Whatever gives rise to the experience of mis-attunement (whether actual or perceived) it is often felt by the client as wounding, hurt, damage, abandonment, or not being heard. Further therapist mis-attunements can compound the hurt, giving rise to self-criticisms, self-attacks, and negative self-judgements, or to confirmations of the client's perceived inadequacy or worthlessness. Mis-attunements are as inevitable in therapy as they are in life, and are part of the ordinary process of coming to shared understandings. Reparation in therapy requires some openness on the part of both persons in the room. In particular, it requires a non-defensive willingness from the therapist to enquire sensitively into the client's felt experience of the actual, or perceived wounding. This openness and willingness to be mutually vulnerable might be considered part of our common humanity or kinship. In the last section of this chapter, we investigate the power of facilitated mediation, when things go badly wrong between client and therapist. It is partly through authentic encounters like this that meaning-making and healing occur.

The role of mediation in resolving complaints

While many mistakes might be dealt with effectively in therapy, others may lead to a complaint being made against the therapist. This is a rare event, but if it does happen it is sometimes possible to resolve problems through the process of facilitated mediation. Whilst mediation is not favoured by all therapeutic professional organisations, it is supported by the UK Council for Psychotherapy (UKCP) as one option in complaint resolution (www.psychotherapy.org.uk/complaints). Mediation might be offered, as a prior step, when a complaint is raised but before it has become fixed in a formal complaint procedure. It might be set up by a training organisation, an accrediting body, or a counselling agency in which the therapist practises. In this section we draw upon our experience of the use of mediation as part of the complaints procedure of the UK Association for Humanistic Psychology Practitioners (UKAHPP).

●●● **Pause for thought: facilitated mediation** ●●●

*Please read the extracts from the UKAHPP complaints procedures, Resource 10
(pp. 117–19). These extracts focus on the role of the facilitators and mediators
within the process. The whole document is available on the UKAHPP website
(www.ahpp.org/ethical/complaints.htm), and you may also wish to refer to this.*

In its use of mediation, this complaints procedure moves beyond the
'super-supervision' of an ethical review, and would be activated *after* the therapeutic relationship has ruptured so badly that communication between the
therapist and the client is failing or non-existent. As you will have seen, each
party to the dispute – client and therapist – is appointed a facilitator, whose role
is to offer a supportive presence both before and during the mediation process.
Facilitated mediation provides an environment where real as well as transferential issues can be explored, and be given consideration and value. For this reason,
mediation should be offered by someone who understands the dynamics of
therapy, who can provide a neutral non-therapy arena to air the issues, and hopefully resolve them in a non-predetermined way (Springwood, 2000: 36–9). The
following vignette illustrates how, even in a less formal voluntary setting, such a
process of mediation is able to address issues between a client and therapist. It
follows the process from the initial complaint to resolution. As you read the
account, there will be some questions for you to pause and consider.

VIGNETTE: 'ANNABEL, EILEEN, ALAN, CANDIDA AND BETH'

After an initial six counselling sessions, Annabel and her client Eileen agree to
'continue for a while longer'. Annabel feels Eileen is revealing more complex difficulties,
and is likely to benefit from ongoing counselling. As Eileen is new to the whole idea of
counselling, Annabel does not want to frighten her away by this suggestion, so she
does not go into the reasons for Eileen continuing counselling.

   After a few months, Eileen is feeling caught in a power dynamic relating to Annabel's
authority. She feels an unidentifiable sense of pressure to continue the counselling.
Sometimes, she cannot bring herself to attend, so calls in to say she is unwell, and then
feels relieved to have a week 'not bothering' with counselling. Annabel names Eileen's
actions as 'acting out' with her non-attendance. Eileen feels told off, but realises she is
behaving irresponsibly. She remains secretly resentful, unable to talk about 'ending', and
what therapy is costing her. Something stops her challenging, since Annabel is so very
caring and concerned when they do meet. Meanwhile, Annabel begins to fear for
Eileen's increasing fragility, and is more apprehensive about mentioning closure.
Eventually, a query about how often Eileen has been ill triggers a row about Annabel 'not
being her doctor too', and leads to Eileen walking out of counselling, angry at Annabel's
increasing 'interference'. She is upset at the break up, but does not want to face going
back and paying money to Annabel to explain her side of things. Six months later, she is
still stewing about the row, and decides to file a complaint about what she sees as
Annabel's 'exploitation' to the Director of the Counselling Centre where Annabel works.

Pause for thought: the meaning of the complaint

- *What do you think the complaint made by Eileen was about, at a surface level, and at a deeper level?*
- *If you were the Director of the Counselling Centre, what would you do next?*
- *Compare your responses with the account which follows.*

Annabel first hears about the complaint via the Centre's Director, Alan, and is deeply shocked. She had been concerned for Eileen, and she had written a letter after the last stormy session to express her hope that one day Eileen might consider resuming therapy 'once her life was on a more even keel, to look at the deeper, developmental issues'. Before the Centre forwards the complaint to her accrediting organisation, Alan suggests he contacts Eileen directly, and over the phone they discuss the nature of her complaint in more detail. Although not claiming that Annabel has been negligent, or actively abusive, Eileen says that she felt 'taken for granted, and out my depth, I wasn't able to see a way out of it all without getting more hurt'. Alan asks: 'Given this difficulty has arisen, what would you like to happen from now on?' Eileen wants some money back for her wasted time, but most of all, wants an apology from Annabel for being so superior and controlling – 'just like my own mother was, stringing me along'. Alan feels that a formal complaint to Annabel's professional organization might not appropriately address these needs, so suggests that they meet with a mediator. Eileen agrees to meet with Annabel provided Alan is present. Annabel also agrees to a meeting. Before the mediation meeting takes place, Annabel has a session with her supervisor, Candida, to explore the issues more fully.

Pause for thought: the supervision session

- *If you were Annabel, how would you prepare for this meeting with your supervisor?*
- *If you were Candida, what issues would you want to explore with Annabel in this session?*

Having thought about these questions, now read what happened next for Annabel and Eileen.

Annabel had wanted to say to Eileen, 'Of course you can decide when to leave, but let's plan this', not to string her along with an open-ended arrangement. She sees how transference and counter-transference issues might have prevented her from being more explicit. The angry departure was reminiscent of Eileen running away from home at age 10, with echoes of her subsequent local authority care, where any questioning protest had led to her being moved on to a new set of foster carers. Annabel knew this history in outline, but also sees how she herself has been controlled by her own fears: predominantly a desire not to confront Eileen with 'the enormous developmental deficit' she saw in such a fragmented upbringing. Once Annabel has taken the opportunity of a 're-visioning' with Candida to recognise her own mishandling of the situation, she can feel less defensive in a meeting with her angry client.

It is agreed that Candida can attend the mediation to support Annabel, while Alan will act as an advocate for the client, since he made a good contact on the phone. Thus the way is paved for the mediation session. Alan, as Centre Director, invites another experienced supervisor, Beth, to act as mediator. She acquaints herself with the situation from each party's supporter beforehand.

●●● *Pause for thought: the mediation meeting* ●●●

- *Imagine this impending mediation meeting. If you are doing this exercise alone, imagine yourself in each person's position – Eileen, the client; Annabel, the therapist; Candida, the supervisor; Alan, the Counselling Centre Director; Beth, the mediator. What might you be thinking and feeling, as each person? What outcome would each person be seeking from the meeting?*
- *If you are able to role-play the meeting with colleagues, or fellow trainees, allow some preparation time before the 'action'. The two pairs – 'Alan' and 'Eileen', and 'Annabel' and 'Candida' – can meet together for 10 or 15 minutes before the mediation meeting is enacted. What might 'Beth' want to do in this time?*
- *Compare your explorations with the following account of how the mediation session actually proceeded.*

The session opens with an immediate apology from Annabel for the misunderstanding about ending. This provides an initial shift, and reframes Annabel's actual authority without it becoming a 'grovelling session', which would merely indulge the therapist and her feelings at the expense of the client's time. After this straightforward apology, Eileen feels able to speak more freely of her feelings of disempowerment, her inability to confront Annabel's authority for reasons she can now well recognise, and her resentment about wasted time and money.

Beth asks which of these issues still has therapeutic import. Annabel and Eileen together reflect on Eileen's childhood of conflicts and break ups, and the lack of any arena in which she could be heard, or in which she could resolve issues. They now share an awareness of how the therapy felt 'interrupted' and unfinished for them both.

Both take a tea break in the mediation session, to allow Annabel to explore with Candida her new awareness of her 'parental' counter-transference of over-concern for continuity. Her own parents had often pressed her to continue with activities when she had in fact wanted to give up. Annabel is able to own her over-concern with continuing on to the end of something. But in this case it has been at the expense of valuing Eileen's adult autonomy. Meanwhile, waiting with Alan, Eileen says she no longer feels the need for financial retribution, since she now appreciates the hours Annabel must have put into thinking about her.

On reconvening, Beth asks both parties what might be their next steps. Eileen wants to resume therapy in her own time, free to come and go. Annabel expresses her continued desire to support Eileen, but is open to checking the 'fusspot' part of herself, in sessions and supervision. So a compromise is agreed. Eileen will resume therapy, after a break to let the dust settle. She will book separate blocks of six sessions, negotiated well in advance. This will make it more financially and emotionally manageable, and both of them will know that Annabel will continue to be present in the background, providing the reparative 'holding' Eileen needs. In the end, each person felt the joy of a creative solution. This was not the way Annabel would previously have imagined working with such a 'needy' client, but when they did resume, it worked well enough for both of them to grow from the experience.

● ● ● *Pause for thought: mistakes, complaints and mediation* ● ● ●

- *How does the above account compare with what you imagined might happen – or what occurred when you used a role-play exploration?*
- *Can you identify some 'ground conditions' for mediation, based on your investigation of this example and any other experience you may have?*

On the surface level, the conflict between Eileen and Annabel concerns a failure in therapeutic contract-making. A formal complaint procedure, centring on this presenting issue alone, may not have reached the deeper transference material. Annabel had never questioned the value of continuity and consistency of care. She had never considered how it might be attached to negative ideas about intrusion or 'power-over'. This had come up against Eileen's fear that we have to take what is offered or receive nothing; in effect be punished for wanting care of a certain kind. The mediator, Beth, could step back enough to identify a mis-attunement and point out styles of relating which they both recognised as part of the misunderstanding.

You will perhaps have identified a number of 'ground conditions' for mediation. There needs to be trust in the goodwill and intent of both participants to seek a resolution, which includes being willing to air the difficulties. This was apparent quite quickly in this case. It was also important here for Alan not to compound the potential mistake by re-entering a therapeutic relationship with the client, but instead to be a listening ear, helping unearth underlying concerns. Mediation is an arena for meta-discourse about the therapy, not to continue it. The focus was on the outcome Eileen was seeking. The mediation process can take some time but it is important to prepare, to give time to be with the difficulty, and not to attempt to move through to a premature closure. Annabel needed time to come to terms with how her actions had been interpreted, and to take responsibility without taking flight into the immobility of shame and guilt.

While other kinds of mediation take place without extra supporters, having a 'buddy' for both parties may be crucial to a successful therapeutic mediation process. While the focus is on practical outcomes, it can then include some handling of emotional content.

At the meeting, structuring time is important: for each not only to put a case, including feelings, thoughts, body responses, and reflection on actions, but also to focus on desirable outcomes. Within mediation, there may be a need for separate sessions or breaks, to come away and reflect on what has been said. In the mediation Annabel made space for her feelings, but did not have to reveal the private story behind them.

In contrast to the preparation period, the actual mediation session moved quickly. We need to be aware that an emotional rather than a legalistic exploration of the dynamics might tempt the parties present to lapse into therapy-session mode. The value of mediation in the presence of third parties is to enable the creative flow of expression between therapist and client to take place without triggering the patterns of the old therapeutic dynamic. The mediator's role is to maintain control of such a dynamic, to keep the emphasis on whatever outcome is mutually desirable at this stage. Explicit reflections on dynamics are in order during the mediation session, to clear the path for a resolution of the unfinished business. Within the healing dynamic of a mediation process, there is both this creative seeking of a new way to relate, and the containing purpose of maintaining the integrity of the therapy contract itself.

Chapter summary

In this chapter we have considered a range of mistakes, mis-attunements, and violations which can occur in therapy, in particular in relation to boundaries, methodology, and the lack of awareness of semi-unconscious transferential processes. We have explored ways in which we might be able to limit such mistakes and find ways of supporting our therapeutic and supervisory practice by seeking assistance from accrediting and registering bodies. Finally, our focus on the stages of mediation provided a critical account of a supportive process that can help in resolving complaints when they arise.

Further reading

Casement, P. (2002) *Learning from our Mistakes: Beyond Dogma in Psychoanalysis and Psychotherapy*. London: Routledge. One of the important themes of this practical book is the need for the therapist to be able to listen, in depth, to their clients.

Kearns, A. (ed.) (2007) *The Mirror Crack'd: When Good Enough Therapy Goes Wrong and other Cautionary Tales for Humanistic Practitioners*. London: Karnac. Relevant chapters from this book include Patti Owens, 'Working through an impasse', pp. 89–104, and Bee Springwood, 'The courage to be human: a humanistic approach to conflict resolution', pp. 125–41.

Kottler, J.A. and Blau, D.S. (1989) *The Imperfect Therapist: Learning from Failure in Therapeutic Practice.* San Francisco, CA and London: Jossey-Bass Publications. This book surveys possible reasons why 'failure' is an inevitable part of being a therapist. It also looks at ways we can learn from our mistakes, using a wide range of reflective, journaling exercises.

Mann, D. (1999) *Psychotherapy: An Erotic Relationship: Transference and Countertransference Passions.* Hove and New York: Routledge. This book is particularly illuminating on how therapists' counter-transference can be separated from other subjective, erotic experiences.

Syme, G. (2003) *Dual Relationships in Counselling and Psychotherapy: Exploring the Limits.* London: Sage. One of the key themes running through this book is relational boundaries. Chapter 9, 'Learning from the boundary riders', is of particular relevance.

CHAPTER 6

REVIEWING YOUR PRACTICE AND LOOKING FORWARD

Conducting a personal and professional practice review

This book has focussed on ethical and creative practice for contemporary therapists. In the vignettes and 'pause for thought' exercises, we have been asking you to reflect on particular issues and specific situations associated with this exploration. Now, in this final chapter, we invite you to review your own personal and professional experience, and to use this review as a basis for making changes or otherwise developing your therapeutic practice. The 'review questionnaire' which follows is divided into five sections, each addressing a different topic, and containing a further series of questions and activities. Only you will be able to work out the responses to these, so we do no more than suggest the matters that you might consider. As with all the questions and exercises in this book, you will probably find it helpful to discuss your responses in supervision or compare your answers with those of a colleague or fellow trainee, depending on the stage of your career and your personal circumstances.

What kind of therapist am I?

Consider what you *bring* to being a therapist:

- in terms of your values, attitudes, beliefs and personal characteristics;
- in the skills, sensitivities and gifts that you know you have developed over your life, including before you became a therapist;
- in those particular areas of understanding and expertise that have grown out of your education, training, personal therapy and experience of being a therapist, so far;
- in any habits, weaknesses, or less helpful propensities to which you think you might be prone.

Consider next what it *means* to you, to be a therapist.

- How does being a therapist fit into the context of your life overall, in terms of convenience, status, enjoyment, or anything else?

- How does your ethical stance as a therapist accord with the values involved in the rest of your life: relationships with family and friends; involvement with other activities or commitments?

- Do you view being a therapist as a job, a vocation, your life's work, a sacred art, a stepping stone to something else, or as some combination of these?

- Consider how you experience being a therapist in the context of community, wider society or culture. What do you think you offer: a desirable commodity, a spiritual contribution, a useful community provision, or something else?

- Consider to what extent being a therapist means taking global issues into account, such as humanitarian and environmental issues. How might these issues impact on you and your clients?

- Think about how the answers you have given to these questions might express or affect your sense of self; your working relationship with clients; your sense of meaning in your life.

How can I take an overview of my practice?

Make a 'map' of your current therapy practice, as follows.

- Start by putting 'yourself' in the middle of a large sheet of paper. Then write your clients' names on the map, positioned to illustrate something about their relationship with you. Alternatively, try making an image to represent each client in your practice, choosing how to place each one on the map. (If you choose to experiment with images, try to represent something significant about the person and their therapy, rather than 'draw their portrait'.)

- Sit with your map – alone or with a colleague – and take in the meaning of the 'practice map' that you have made.

- Take some time to note, for example, any clients you feel concerned about, those who take up extra mental space outside the therapy hour, those with whom the work feels 'easy', any clients you realise you tend not to bring to supervision, and anything else of significance.

- Maybe over a series of peer study or supervision sessions, use your map to think about the relationship you have with each of your clients, and the work that is going on currently with them. Notice if there are any potentially significant *patterns* of relationship and ask for support for you to become more aware of any transferential issues these patterns may reveal.

- Review the balance of your practice. Maybe there are things you would like to change about such matters as the range of clients you see, the opportunities to push your 'growing edge' a bit, the contexts you might work in. You might want to make another 'map'. This time place your work as therapist with clients in the centre, then add the supports you have, or need to put in place; areas of interest you want to pursue; growing edges to consider.

How do I balance safety and creativity in my everyday practice?

Review your ways of making therapeutic agreements, or contracts, with clients.

- Do you make explicit contracts with clients, as a general rule? If so, look over any written agreements, or lists of initial discussion points, that you currently use. Do you want to change anything about the wording or the process you usually go through with a new client? If not, examine the reasons why you do not make explicit contracts – is this your active choice?

- Consider any client who might be coming to a stage in their therapy where it might be in order to review therapeutic aims, processes or boundaries, at this point – maybe because of a change of focus or an impending end of therapy. Is it possible to think of a way to do this creatively, with that particular client in mind?

Look at the therapeutic environment you are providing for your clients.

- Think of your most vulnerable client. Does the environmental frame you have made for therapy provide them with as much security, confidentiality and containment as possible?

- Does this environment sustain your creativity as a therapist? Are there enough satisfying moments of discovery with clients, or moments when you can risk being in the unknown with them?

- Can you think of ways of giving this therapeutic space more potential for creativity? (Think about times when you might value having some objects or materials in the room, for instance.)

- Does your practice help clients reconnect to their life beyond therapy?

Take some time to review your personal and professional self-care and development.

- How do you take care of yourself as a therapist? For instance, what do you do when fatigued or when your energy is low?

- To what extent has all your training so far offered you an ethical grounding? Do you feel you need a more secure base from which to develop your practice? Do you want to experiment with new ways of being with clients? How much has training stretched you to try new experiences of yourself individually and within a group? Are there depths you fear falling into?

- Reflect on the regularity, timing, content and style of your supervision arrangements. Is this really giving you the opportunity effectively to 're-vision' your work with clients and make sure you feel as professionally grounded as possible? Is there anything you might need to change in this area?

- Consider whether you yourself might benefit from some more, or different personal therapy experience – maybe because something has changed or emerged in your own life, or been triggered by client work touching a new issue for you.

- Do you find enough time to read, reflect and study? If appropriate, consider how this aspect of your development might be better supported. Maybe find or initiate a peer study group? Go more often to see films, art or plays? Think of other ways in which you might support your all-round development as a therapist and a person.

- Think about further training or professional development. Do you feel you need more training to keep you engaged with the work you do? Do you find yourself going to events you feel you 'ought' to go to, rather than ones you feel really engaged in? Is there something you would be really interested to find out more about? How can you follow this up?

- What is the right balance between work, rest and play for you? Is there something you need to adjust to restore an ethical and creative balance?

How well supported would I be if something went wrong?

Review your therapeutic executor arrangements.

- Have you already arranged for a trusted person to be your therapeutic executor? If the answer is no, should you not try to begin the process of finding someone to take this responsibility? If the answer is yes, you might wish to take some time to make sure that the arrangements you have made are as secure and easy to implement as possible. Look again at the sample guidelines about setting up such an arrange- ment in Resource 9 (pp. 115–16). Your professional organisation might also have some suitable advice to give you.

Consider circumstances where you might need to seek an 'ethical review' of some aspect of your practice.

- Look again at the ethical review procedure outlined in Chapter 5 (p. 88). If you needed someone 'outside' your current professional circle to act as a consultant or ethical reviewer, where would you turn to for help?

Think about the support that might be there for you and your client, should a dispute, conflict, crisis or complaint arise.

- Familiarise yourself again with the ethical codes and complaints procedures used by your professional organisation. Do the values expressed and behaviours expected accord closely enough with your own values and expectations? If not, what will you do about this?

- If you work in an organisational setting, consider whether the ethical considerations you have identified sit comfortably with the policies and procedures of the agency within which you operate. If not, what will you do about it?

- What range of supports is offered by your professional association and your insurance company to assist you, your client and your supervisor in the event of a dispute or complaint? Do these seem adequate to you? If not, what will you do about it?

Am I developing practical wisdom as a therapist?

Consider the summary given below of some of the main features of a therapist's practical wisdom, as discussed in this book. Are there other features you would add? Which ones are most important to you, do you think?

- Practical wisdom involves us as therapists in holding a balance between safety and creativity in our work with clients. This is at the heart of ethical and effective therapeutic practice, a practice which is both a science and an art.

- Our practical wisdom as therapists arises from and is embedded in the experience of therapeutic work and relationship. That work nevertheless takes place in a social, political, cultural and spiritual setting, affecting both client and therapist.

- Practical wisdom enables us to recognise that the contexts for therapy can sometimes limit possibilities, sometimes expand and enhance possibilities, but will always have an impact, and we take responsibility for the amount of security and creativity a particular context might provide.

- Part of our practical wisdom comes from the knowledge that the therapeutic relationship has a number of levels or dimensions, including the transferential. When therapists and clients experience the effects of 'transferring' emotions and relational expectations into the therapeutic relationship, as therapists we need a sharpened ethical awareness and as much creativity and openness as we can muster.

- Theory informs practice and practice informs theory; reflective practice – both personal reflection and reflection with others – supports practical wisdom. Yet we understand that knowledge is provisional and therapists will hold 'not knowing' as well as the things they know from learning, experience and reflection.

- Therapists practising ethically will often need to hold and balance a number of competing values and practical demands. Practically wise therapists try to hold the whole – not splitting or discarding whatever does not fit with a preconceived view.

- In exercising practical wisdom, we look for movement and resolution more than an expedient 'solution' – a process of decision making involving both client and therapist which can be owned and shared. This is linked to our preference for non-defensive openness in the exploration of 'negative' issues with clients, bearing our own vulnerability at such times, in order to work through to a resolution.

Lastly, review your own development of 'practical wisdom'.

- To what extent does your own practice exemplify or illustrate some of the features of practical wisdom listed above?

- Are any of these features ones that you would like to develop further, with the aim of enriching creativity and securing your work on a more ethical basis? How might you go about supporting this development?

In conclusion, we hope you will have found carrying out this review helpful in evaluating your practice in terms of the book's themes, and as a basis for your future development as a therapist.

RESOURCE 1

Card index summary

Client/supervisee

[Some categories apply to clients only.]

Name:

Address:

Email:

Tel: (h)   **(m)**   **(wk)**

[indicate where messages can be left]

Date of birth:

Referrer:

GP's address and phone number: [including emergency phone number]

Initial contact date: **Contract signed:**

First therapy session date: **Fee:** [includes dates when fees are re-negotiated]

Final therapy session date:

Code number: [for split record systems]

[reverse side of the index card is an accumulative record of session dates]

RESOURCE 2

Initial meeting and assessment proforma

Name:

Address:

Telephone: [indicate preferred mode of contact]   **Email:**

Referred by:

Agreement signed: [this might include frequency, duration, agreed review periods, boundaries around confidentiality, fees, focus, goals, etc.]

CORE form completed: [if appropriate]

Appearance:

Reason for wanting psychotherapy:

Presenting problems and their duration:

Precipitating factors:

Current conflicts (and further problems):

Underlying conflicts (and past problems):

Criteria for change:

Possible approaches:

Offer and responses:

Significant names, relationships (including losses), places mentioned by client, and family tree. Date any updates to this initial information:

Outcome (refer to criteria for change):

Correspondence (attached):   **code no:** [for split records only]

RESOURCE 3

Process session notes proforma

[These notes, which do not identify clients, should be kept in a separate journal or folder.]

Date: time/duration: missed appts: code no: [for split records only]

Content: [summary of client's narrative, manner, behaviour, feelings, and therapist's interventions. Also themes, transference/counter-transference, significant dreams, etc.]

Process: [any comments made by client about the process, therapist's observations and/or speculations about the process]

Family: [information from here might be used to update Initial Meeting and Assessment Proforma information]

Literature given:

Notes for next session: [e.g. any agreement about what client or therapist would do between sessions, issues to be reviewed during the session or for the therapist to be aware of]

Issues for supervision:

Issues for own therapy:

Notes about any correspondence or telephone conversations:

RESOURCE 4

Process session notes – an example

Date: 23 May 2011 **Time/duration:** 60 mins **Session No:** 10 **Code No:** AB0511

Content: [e.g. summary of client's narrative, manner, behaviour, feelings, and therapist's interventions. Themes, e.g. transference/counter-transference, significant dreams, etc.]

A. spoke about depression again, and how the origins of this began when he was 24 years old (four years ago), and after the sudden loss of his father. Spoke about what his father meant to him. Felt quite emotional with statements like: 'He will never see how my life turned out'; 'I want him to know that I haven't disappointed him'.

I stayed close to his feelings and his grief throughout the session. I was aware that he might possibly be beginning to view me as a father figure in the transference. I felt fatherly towards him, as if he were six years old. I enquired about his early life experiences with this father. A. remarked that he was 'daddy's boy' up until the age of seven when 'father accepted a job abroad, but the family remained behind in the UK'. Exploration of what this was like for a seven year old. A. remarked how grief stricken he had been, and although he knew that his father would be returning in six months this time period felt like eternity for him. He also remarked that he had to be the 'brave boy for his mother' who was frequently upset by the father's absence. I said: 'It sounds as if the little boy in you had to hide his tears'. At this point A. became very upset. I felt strong fatherly counter-transference feelings at that point, and imagined that A. became the little boy in that moment. I stayed close to his feelings throughout.

Process: [comments made by client about the process, therapist's observations and/or speculations about the process]

A. remarked how he felt lighter at the end of the session, and that he had not cried so much in years, 'perhaps ever'. It feels as if he is grieving the double loss of his father; both at seven and 24 years old.

Family: Mother consumed with sadness when father went to work abroad when A. was seven.

Literature/web-links/other information given: N/A.

Notes for next session: [e.g. any agreement about what client or therapist would do between sessions, issues to be reviewed during the session or for the therapist to be aware of]
    N/A other than to remain with whatever A. brings to the session.

Issues for supervision: Explore transference and counter-transference issues. Perhaps voice fact of my own loss of father at the age of 22.

Issues for own therapy:

Notes about any correspondence or telephone conversations: N/A

RESOURCE 5

Contract example A

Health centre counselling contract

Dear Patient,

You have been referred by _____ (GP) for some counselling sessions to help you deal with matters discussed recently.

Your first appointment is on _____.

Your counsellor is _____.

You will have _____ sessions of 50 minutes. These are the dates:

1.   2.
3.   4.
5.   6.

Notes

- Please try to arrive promptly for your appointment.
- Wait for your counsellor in the reception area as usual.
- Sessions last 50 minutes. If you arrive late sessions will still finish on time as other patients should not be kept waiting.
- If you are unable to attend for any reason please ring the health centre in advance to let your counsellor know.
- Any sessions you miss will still be counted as part of the series of sessions that you have been allocated.
- All records associated with your counselling are subject to the Data Protection and Freedom of Information Acts.

Yours sincerely,

(Counsellor)

RESOURCE 6

Contract example B

Psychotherapy contract

This agreement expresses the commitment each of us makes at the outset. Once we have discussed and agreed the details, we will each sign and keep one copy to register our shared understanding.

1 We have agreed to meet weekly on _____ at _____. This is an open-ended therapy contract which can be reviewed at any time. We will check in with each other periodically to see how you are experiencing the process.

2 Your therapy appointment is 'your time' each week that I have set aside for you. Each session lasts one hour. It is important for effective therapy that we try to maintain a regular commitment. If a change of circumstance makes this difficult for you, we can discuss the possibility of a different date and time and I will do my best to rearrange things if I can.

3 The fee we have agreed is £_____ per one hour session. Fees are due each session/on the last session of each month. Fees will rise from time to time and I will give you adequate notice of this.

4 I will be ready for you at the appointed time. Please try to arrive on time as I do not have a waiting room. If you arrive late for any reason the session will still finish at the appointed time.

5 I will take all reasonable precautions to keep our therapy space safe from interruption and intrusion, such as from telephone calls, deliveries and workmen, though there may be rare occasions when this is not feasible. I ask you to respect the therapy space too, as far as possible.

6 You have my phone number in case you need it. My telephone answering machine will usually be on if I am not available when you call.

7 Please avoid taking mind-altering drugs or alcohol before a session.

8 I will take holidays during the year – usually in the summer period, at Christmas/New Year, and Easter/Passover, plus 'half term' weeks where appropriate. I will let you know the dates well in advance. If you decide to take a holiday yourself please

let me know at least four weeks in advance. I will then only charge you half the usual fee for sessions missed. If you give me less notice than this, I will expect you to pay the full fee for any missed sessions.

9   If you are unable to attend a session due to unforeseen circumstances, please call and let me know, and we may be able to re-schedule. Please bear in mind, however, that such re-arrangement may not always be possible. My flexibility is limited by the fact that I see most clients on a regular basis, at the same time and day each week, so alternative appointment times are not freely available.

10   The therapeutic relationship is intended to be a healing, supportive and sometimes challenging relationship. We need to be aware that there may be times, as in any human relationship, when things feel difficult and it seems hard to persevere. These times, if worked through together, can be very fruitful. We both need to have the intention of seeing things through in such circumstances.

11   If either of us thinks it is time to bring the therapy to an end, we will discuss this together and decide if and how to do that. Sometimes one session is enough to make sure the decision is a good one. Sometimes it is better to have a series of sessions to review the work, and decide either to go on with therapy after all, or else find a way of making a good ending for you. Ending the therapeutic relationship should ideally be a mutual experience and not a one-sided or impulsive act.

12   Everything that happens in our therapy session remains confidential between us, with the following exceptions:

- I may discuss aspects of our work for supervisory or other professional purposes but your identity will in all circumstances remain completely protected.
- when required by law, which is very rare; for this reason, I will keep a copy of this contract and a record of your attendance for seven years from the date of termination of therapy.
- I may contact your GP or any other appropriate professional if I believe there is a serious risk to yourself or others.

Therapeutic issues we have identified at the outset:

Further comments (if appropriate):

Signed.. (client)

Date..

Signed.. (therapist)

Date..

RESOURCE 7

Contract example C

Hillside Therapy Centre: client agreement

Please read this before you attend your first therapy session

All our therapists are registered members of the BACP, UKCP or HPC.

You are considering entering into an open-ended therapy contract. This means that you are undertaking to make space in your life for personal growth and change. Your therapist will make a commitment to support you in this endeavour. At the first meeting you will talk about the approach your therapist uses and be able to reflect on its suitability for you.

After an initial session to discuss your reasons for seeking therapy at this time and to ensure that therapy seems the right option for you, you will undertake to meet with your therapist at a regular time and day each week/fortnight/month.

The process of therapy will be reviewed from time to time. Sometimes this will lead to a change of emphasis or focus; sometimes it will mark the end of one phase of therapy and begin a new one; at a later point you will discuss ending the therapy. Therapy continues only by mutual agreement between you and your therapist.

We ask you to arrive on time for your appointment as the session will always finish on time, even if you are late. If you arrive early, there is a waiting room where you can make a hot drink and use the toilet if you wish.

If you know that you are going to miss a session, or if you are going to be late, please ring the centre if possible before the session is due to start. Our normal policy is to charge a cancellation fee for unplanned missed sessions. Your therapist will discuss this with you at the first meeting.

Please make a note here of your reasons for seeking therapy and what you hope to gain from the experience. Thank you.

RESOURCE 8

Contract example D

Jones & Co. employee assistance programme
About your counselling

Dear Employee,

Following your recent interview with a manager from Human Resources Dept. you are being referred for_____ sessions with a counsellor.

Please complete the attached questionnaire and return to:

_____ (counsellor)

At

_____

_____

_____ (address)

Your appointment dates are as follows:

1.

2.

3.

4.

5.

6.

7.

8.

Yours faithfully,

Counselling questionnaire

Make some notes about these questions and discuss your responses with your counsellor at the first appointment.

1 Why are you having counselling?

2 How do you think counselling might help you in your job?

3 What are your objectives over the eight sessions?

You will be asked to complete a client feedback form when you have completed the series of counselling sessions. This will be sent to the Human Resources Dept. and used as the basis for your 'improving performance' interview.

RESOURCE 9

Therapeutic executor – UKAHPP guidelines

The UKAHPP strongly recommends that all members in practice have a therapeutic executor, and this is a requirement for all accredited/full members.

A therapeutic executor is a person who deals with the closure of a member's practice in the event of the member's death. The death of a therapist or counsellor may have a profound effect on his/her clients – at the very least, clients have to be informed, future sessions cancelled and supervision/insurance/membership/consulting room arrangements terminated. In the same way that the making of a will is a responsible act and a caring act for one's family, the arrangement of a therapeutic executor is a professionally responsible and caring act for one's client.

The UKAHPP suggests that one's partner or close family member, who would have to deal with the emotional and practical family-centred consequences of one's death, may not be the best person to also act as one's therapeutic executor; a close friend may also find it too emotionally difficult. If partners or close family members are therapeutic executors there may also be unknown or unexpected boundary issues in dealing with one's clients, especially regarding confidentiality. It may well be that a professional colleague would be better placed, both professionally and emotionally, to communicate with clients in such circumstances. However, as such circumstances vary widely and the choice of a therapeutic executor is a private and personal matter, the UKAHPP presents this not as a requirement but as advice only, for every member's consideration in choosing who could best act as therapeutic executor (and the AHPP does not intend to enquire into such arrangements).

What is required for a therapeutic executor arrangement to work well is that:

1. the member maintains a list of every client's contact details (their address as well as phone or email) and a diary of future appointments; this has to be kept up-to-date;

2. 'clients' should include both therapy-clients and supervisees; additionally, the ability to contact professional bodies, colleagues, trainees, etc. would be helpful for the therapeutic executor;

3. the member's therapeutic executor knows where to access the contact-list and diary, and has written consent from the member to do this;

4 further arrangements have been discussed and agreed for the therapeutic executor to access and dispose of all files and notes on clients and client-sessions;

5 the extent of the therapeutic executor's role has been discussed and agreed; minimally it should start with informing clients, and might extend to offering support (and/or sessions), helping to find new therapists, informing insurers etc., dealing with the financial side of the member's practice . . . One major issue that has arisen in some cases is whether clients can attend the funeral.

6 all these arrangements have to be made with due regard to confidentiality; for example, the therapeutic executor should know how and where to access this information in the event of the member's death, but probably should not have prior access to it.

7 the member's partner/immediate family should be aware of who is the therapeutic executor, and that this person will be taking care these matters.

One possibility is that acting as a therapeutic executor can be a reciprocal arrangement between two UKAHPP members, or between colleagues whether or not they are both members. Another possibility is that this becomes part of a long-term supervision arrangement. A lot of time and emotional energy can be involved – probably more than expected; one AHPP member who acted as therapeutic executor for another member with quite a small practice concluded that she would not ask someone to be her therapeutic executor without arranging some remuneration from her estate.

Although we are all tempted to postpone making wills and may also prefer to avoid these 'intimations of mortality' in relation to our professional practice, the UKAHPP believes that arranging a therapeutic executor is a responsible, humanistic and caring act in relation both to our families and our clients.

RESOURCE 10

Extracts from the UKAHPP complaints procedure

A full and up-to-date version of the document from which these extracts have been taken can be found at www.ahpp.org/ethical/complaints.htm

Once a complaint is received the procedure follows the stages summarised below

1 Appointment of coordinator, facilitators and mediator – the ethics officer receives a copy of the complaint from the general secretary. The ethics officer appoints a complaint coordinator (or acts as the coordinator) to oversee the complaint and appoints facilitators to assist the parties involved.

2 Facilitation – the complainant is offered a facilitator to assist them to clarify the nature of the complaint in terms of UKAHPP's Codes of Ethics and of Practice. The complainant is encouraged to use the mediation process to resolve the complaint. If the complainant agrees, the member complained against is then informed of the complaint, offered their own facilitator to assist them and encouraged to participate in mediation. If either party is not willing to proceed to mediation the formal complaint procedure is implemented.

3 Mediation – If both parties agree to mediation they and their facilitators meet with an independent mediator appointed by the ethics officer. If, as a result of mediation, a resolution acceptable to both parties is agreed the case is closed. If resolution is not achieved the formal complaint procedure is implemented.

[…]

Facilitation and mediation stage (before making a formal complaint)

Facilitation

1 The complainant is contacted by a facilitator (a member of UKAHPP who has no relationship with the member complained against) to offer confidential help and support in making their complaint. Such support can be advice on the procedures

involved and help in formulating what the complainant may wish to say in the meetings that follow. Complainant and facilitator explore the possibility of resolving the issue by mediation, prior to entering the lengthy formal complaints procedure.

2   This facilitation process is confidential with the identity of the complainant and member complained against known only to the general secretary, ethics officer, complaint coordinator and facilitator at this stage. If it is necessary to discuss the complaint within UKAHPP the identities of the parties involved are not revealed. As the object of this process is in part to determine whether a complaint would be appropriate, the member complained against will not necessarily be informed of the complaint until mediation is sought or a formal complaint entered.

3   Should the complainant choose to proceed, the member complained against is informed of the complaint. The member is allocated their own facilitator to support them through mediation or the complaints procedure. If both parties agree to mediation, the ethics officer appoints a mediator who may be a member of UKAHPP but with no connection with the member complained against. If mediation is rejected by either party, or is deemed inappropriate, the formal complaints procedure is implemented instead.

   a   If the person complained against is no longer a member of UKAHPP (resignations are not permitted while a complaint is in progress) the matter cannot be handled by UKAHPP as an official complaint. However, the ex-member will be encouraged to attend a mediation process. If they refuse UKAHPP cannot take the process any further. The complainant can be advised alternative courses of action, such as a complaint to a professional body of which the person complained about is a member.

Mediation

1   The complaints coordinator arranges a mediation meeting, which the parties and their facilitators attend. This meeting is to take place within sixty (60) days of the appointment of the mediator. In the event that the parties are unable to agree a date for this meeting within the time limit the mediation process is deemed to have lapsed and the formal complaints procedure will be implemented (as long as the member is a member of UKAHPP).

   a   The mediator receives from the coordinator all the relevant information about the complaint. At the meeting the role of the mediator is to help the parties clarify their issues and reach a satisfactory outcome. The mediator first hears from the complainant, then from the member, and allows comments of clarification from the facilitators. This initial expression of views is heard without interruption or contradiction. Time is then given for responses to this initial round, and for the complainant and the member to put forward their wishes for a satisfactory outcome. If no agreement can be reached at this stage, then one future meeting will be arranged.

b   If agreement is reached after one or two meetings, the mediator documents in writing the agreed resolution and any agreed future action for either or both parties, together with a time scale or date for completion. Both sign this document and a copy is sent to them. If future actions within a time scale have been agreed then the complaint coordinator is informed when they're completed, or they are pursued if defaulted upon. The complaint is then deemed resolved.

c   Alternatively, if no agreement can be reached this is recorded in writing by the mediator and signed by both parties and a copy sent to them. The formal complaints procedure is then implemented, as long as the member is a current member of UKAHPP, or unless the complainant wishes to withdraw the complaint.

2   The mediator's report is filed by the ethics officer, but any other documents or other records used or created during the mediation stage are destroyed or returned to the relevant 'owning' individuals, even if a formal complaint is to be pursued. If a formal complaint procedure is to follow the mediator cannot be involved, but the complainant's and the member's facilitators may continue with these roles.

REFERENCES

Abram, D. (1997) *The Spell of the Sensuous: Perception and Language in a More-Than-Human World.* New York: Pantheon Books.

Abram, D. (2010) *Becoming Animal: An Earthly Cosmology.* New York: Pantheon Books.

Abrams, S. and Neubauer, P.B. (1978) 'Transitional objects: animate and inanimate', in S.A. Grolnick and L. Barkin (eds), *Between Reality and Fantasy: Transitional Objects and Phenomena.* New York and London: Jason Aronson. pp. 133–44.

Anderson, S.K. and Handelsman, M.M. (2010) *Ethics for Psychotherapists and Counsellors: A Proactive Approach.* Chichester: Wiley-Blackwell.

Aristotle (1976) *The Ethics of Aristotle*, trans. J.A.K. Thomson. Harmondsworth: Penguin.

Asheri, S. (2009) 'To touch or not to touch: a relational body psychotherapy perspective', in L. Hartley (ed.), *Contemporary Body Psychotherapy: The Chiron Approach.* London: Routledge. pp. 106–20.

BACP (British Association for Counselling and Psychotherapy) (2007) *Ethical Framework for Good Practice in Counselling and Psychotherapy.* Lutterworth: BACP.

Beebe, J. (2005) *Integrity in Depth.* College Station: Texas A&M University Press.

Binder, P., Holgersen, H. and Nielsen, G. (2009) 'Why did I change when I went to therapy? A qualitative analysis of former patients' conceptions of successful psychotherapy', *Counselling & Psychotherapy Research*, 9 (4): 250–6.

Bond, T. (2010) *Standards and Ethics for Counselling in Action* (3rd edn). London: Sage.

Bond, T. and Mitchels, B. (2008) *Confidentiality and Record Keeping in Counselling and Psychotherapy.* London: Sage.

Bowlby, J. (2003) *A Secure Base: Clinical Applications of Attachment Theory.* London: Brunner-Routledge.

Casement, P. (1985) *On Learning from the Patient.* London: Routledge.

Casement, P. (1990) *Further Learning from the Patient: The Analytic Space and Process.* London: Routledge.

Casement, P. (2002) *Learning from our Mistakes: Beyond Dogma in Psychoanalysis and Psychotherapy.* London: Routledge.

Casemore, R. (ed.) (2001) *Surviving Complaints against Counsellors and Psychotherapists: Towards Understanding and Healing.* Ross-on-Wye: PCCS Books.

Clarkson, P. (1995) *Gestalt Counselling in Action.* London: Sage.

Cooper, M. (2010) 'The challenge of counselling and psychotherapy research', *Counselling & Psychotherapy Research*, 10 (3): 183–91.

Eiden, B. (2002) 'Application of post-Reichian body psychotherapy', in T. Staunton (ed.), *Body Psychotherapy.* Hove: Brunner-Routledge. pp. 27–55.

Fox, S. (2008) *Relating to Clients: The Therapeutic Relationship for Complementary Therapists.* London and Philadelphia, PA: Jessica Kingsley.

Gabriel, L. (2005) *Speaking the Unspeakable: The Ethics of Dual Relationships in Counselling and Psychotherapy*. London and New York: Routledge.

Gabriel, L. and Casemore, R. (eds) (2009) *Relational Ethics in Practice: Narratives from Counselling and Psychotherapy*. London: Routledge.

Germer, C. (2009) *The Mindful Path to Self-Compassion*. New York and London: Guilford Press.

Gilbert, P. (2009) *Compassion Focussed Therapy*. London: Routledge.

Gilhooley, D. (2011) 'Mistakes', *Psychoanalytic Psychology*, 28 (2): 311–33.

Gray, A. (1994) *An Introduction to the Therapeutic Frame*. London and New York: Routledge.

Grof, S. (2000) *Psychology of the Future: Lessons from Modern Consciousness Research*. New York: State University of New York Press.

Hartley, L. (ed.) (2009) *Contemporary Body Psychotherapy: The Chiron Approach*. London: Routledge.

Hyde, L. (2007) *The Gift: How the Creative Spirit Transforms the World*. Edinburgh: Canongate.

Jenkins, P. (2007) *Counselling, Psychotherapy and the Law* (2nd edn). London: Sage.

Johnson, S.M. (1994) *Character Styles*. New York and London: W. W. Norton.

Kalmanowitz, D. and Lloyd, B. (1997) *The Portable Studio: Art Therapy and Political Conflict*. London: Health Education Authority.

Kearns, A. (2005) *The Seven Deadly Sins? Issues in Clinical Practice and Supervision for Humanistic and Integrative Practitioners*. London: Karnac.

Kearns, A. (ed.) (2007) *The Mirror Crack'd: When Good Enough Therapy Goes Wrong and Other Cautionary Tales for Humanistic Practitioners*. London: Karnac.

Khele, S., Symons, C. and Wheeler, S. (2008) 'An analysis of complaints to the British Association for Counselling and Psychotherapy, 1996–2006', *Counselling and Psychotherapy Research*, 8 (2): 124–32.

Klein, M. (1975) *Envy and Gratitude and Other Works 1946–1963*. London: Hogarth Press and Institute of Psycho-Analysis.

Knox, R. and Cooper, M. (2011) 'A state of readiness: an exploration of the client's role in meeting at relational depth', *Journal of Humanistic Psychology*, 51 (1): 61–81.

Kottler, J.A. and Blau, D.S. (1989) *The Imperfect Therapist: Learning from Failure in Therapeutic Practice*. San Francisco, CA and London: Jossey-Bass Publications.

Lee, R.G. (ed.) (2004) *The Values of Connection: A Relational Approach to Ethics*. Cambridge, MA: Gestalt Press.

Lendrum, S. (2004) 'Satisfactory endings in therapeutic relationships, Part 2', *Healthcare, Counselling and Psychotherapy Journal*, 4 (3): 31–5.

Lichner Ingram, B. (2011) *Clinical Case Formulations: Matching the Integrative Treatment Plan to the Client* (3rd edn). London: Wiley.

Lomas, P. (1999) *Doing Good? Psychotherapy Out of its Depth*. Oxford: Oxford University Press.

Macaro, A. (2006) *Reason, Virtue and Psychotherapy*. Chichester: Whurr Publishers.

Mann, D. (1999) *Psychotherapy: An Erotic Relationship: Transference and Countertransference Passions*. Hove and New York: Routledge.

McLeod, J. and Machin, L. (1998) 'The context of counselling: a neglected dimension of training, research and practice', *British Journal of Guidance and Counselling*, 26 (3): 325–36.

McNiff, S. (2004) *Art Heals: How Creativity Cures the Soul*. Boston, MA and London: Shambhala.

Mindell, A. (2010) *Processmind: A User's Guide to Connecting with the Mind of God*. Wheaton, IL: Quest.

Mitchels, B. and Bond, T. (2010) *Essential Law for Counsellors and Psychotherapists*. London: Sage.

Mollon, P. (2002) *Shame and Jealousy: The Hidden Turmoils*. London: Karnac.

Monk-Steel, J. (2009) 'The complaints process from the perspective of the individual registrant', in *Safer Practice Guidance for Psychotherapists*. Internal publication by the Ethics Committee of the Karuna Institute and the Association of Core Process Psychotherapists.

Neff, K. (2011) *Self-Compassion: Stop Beating Yourself Up and Leave Insecurity Behind*. New York: William Morrow.

Nhat Hanh, T. (2010) *Reconciliation: Healing the Inner Child*. Berkeley, CA: Parallax Press.

Nicholas, M.W. (1994) *The Mystery of Goodness (and the Positive Moral Consequences of Psychotherapy)*. New York and London: W. W. Norton.

O'Brien, M. and Houston, G. (2004) *Integrative Therapy: A Practitioner's Guide*. London: Sage.

Orbach, S. (2000) *The Impossibility of Sex*. London: Penguin.

Owens, P. (2007a) 'Humanistic therapy contracts: good for clients and therapists?', *Self and Society*, 34 (5): 34–43.

Owens, P. (2007b) 'Benign revelation: writing about work with clients', *Self and Society*, 35 (1): 20–9.

Palmer-Barnes, F. (1998) *Complaints and Grievances in Psychotherapy*. London and New York: Routledge.

Philippson, P. (2001) *Self in Relation*. New York: Gestalt Journal Press.

Proctor, B. (2002) *The Dynamics of Power in Counselling and Psychotherapy: Ethics, Politics and Practice*. Ross-on-Wye: PCCS Books.

Rothschild, B. (2006) *Help for the Helper: The Psychophysiology of Compassion Fatigue and Vicarious Trauma*. New York and London: W. W. Norton.

Rowan, J. and Jacobs, M. (2002) *The Therapist's Use of Self*. Milton Keynes: Open University Press.

Russell, J. (1993) *Out of Bounds: Sexual Exploitation in Counselling and Therapy*. London: Sage.

Schaverien, J. (1997), 'Men who leave too soon: reflections on the erotic transference and countertransference', *British Journal of Psychotherapy*, 14 (1): 3–15.

Seinfeld, J. (1990) *The Bad Object: Handling the Negative Therapeutic Reaction in Psychotherapy*. New Jersey and London: Jason Aronson.

Shaw, R. (2003) *The Embodied Psychotherapist: The Therapist's Body Story*. Hove and New York: Brunner-Routledge.

Sills, C. (ed.) (2006) *Contracts in Counselling and Psychotherapy*. London, Sage.

Sprang, G., Clark, J.J. and Whitt-Woosley, A. (2007) 'Compassion fatigue, compassion satisfaction, and burnout: factors impacting a professional's quality of life', *Journal of Loss and Trauma*, 12 (3): 259–80.

Springwood, B. (2000) 'AHPP mediation philosophy', *Self and Society*, 28 (1): 36–9.

Spurling, L. (2009) *An Introduction to Psychodynamic Counselling* (2nd edn). Basingstoke and New York: Palgrave Macmillan.

Staunton, T. (2002) 'Sexuality and body psychotherapy', in T. Staunton (ed.) *Body Psychotherapy*. Hove: Brunner-Routledge. pp. 56–77.

Stern, D.N. (1985) *The Interpersonal World of the Infant: A View from Psychoanalysis and Developmental Psychology*. New York: Basic Books.

Stern, D.N. (2004) *The Present Moment in Psychotherapy and Everyday Life*. New York: W. W. Norton.

Syme, G. (2003) *Dual Relationships in Counselling and Psychotherapy: Exploring the Limits.* London: Sage.

Totton, N. (2010) *The Problem with Humanistic Psychotherapies.* London: Karnac.

Waska, R. (2008). 'Using countertransference: analytic contact, projective identification, and transference phantasy states', *American Journal of Psychotherapy*, 62 (4): 333–51.

Winnicott, D.W. (1958) *Collected Papers: Through Pediatrics to Psychoanalysis.* New York: Basic Books.

Winnicott, D.W. (1971) *Playing and Reality.* Harmondsworth: Penguin.

Winnicott, D.W. (1986) *Home Is Where We Start From.* Harmondsworth: Penguin.

Winnicott, D.W. (1990) *The Maturational Processes and the Facilitating Environment: Studies in the Theory of Emotional Development.* London: Karnac Books and the Institute of Psycho-Analysis.

Wosket, V. (1999) *The Therapeutic Use of Self: Counselling Practice, Research and Supervision.* London: Brunner-Routledge.

Zinker, J. (1978) *Creative Process in Gestalt Therapy.* New York: Vintage.

INDEX